VGM Opportunities Series

OPPORTUNITIES IN
MEDICAL IMAGING
CAREERS

Clifford J. Sherry, Ph.D.

Revised Edition

Foreword by
Robert S. Ledley
Chairman
Computerized Medical Imaging Society

VGM Career Horizons
NTC/Contemporary Publishing Group

Library of Congress Cataloging-in-Publication Data

Sherry, Clifford J.
    Opportunities in medical imaging careers / Clifford J. Sherry ; foreword by
Robert S. Ledley. — Rev. ed.
        p. cm. — (VGM opportunities series)
    Includes bibliographical references.
    ISBN 0-658-00196-5 (cloth) — ISBN 0-658-00197-3 (paperback)
        1. Diagnositc imaging—Vocational guidance.   2. Medical technologists—
Vocational guidance.   I. Title.   II. Series.
    RC78.7.D53 S45   2000
    616.07'54'023—dc21   99-53371
                                                                                                    CIP

Cover photograph: © PhotoDisc, Inc.

Published by VGM Career Horizons
A division of NTC/Contemporary Publishing Group, Inc.
4255 West Touhy Avenue, Lincolnwood (Chicago), Illinois 60712-1975 U.S.A.
Copyright © 2000 by NTC/Contemporary Publishing Group, Inc.
Printed in the United States of America
International Standard Book Number: 0-658-00196-5 (cloth)
                                                                     0-658-00197-3 (paper)

00 01 02 03 04 05 LB 15 14 13 12 11 10 9   8   7   6   5   4   3   2   1

DEDICATION

This book is dedicated to my aunts and uncles—

Anton and Janet Odehnal
Joseph and Elaine Falout

and to my cousins—

Doreen Odehnal
Joseph Falout

CONTENTS

About the Author viii

Foreword x

Acknowledgments. xii

Introduction xiii

1. What Would Have Happened?. 1

Moving X rays. Improvements. Computed tomographic
scanner: a new approach. Magnetic resonance imaging.
Ultrasonics. Medical ultrasonic imaging. Doppler ultrasonic
scanners. Functional imaging. Safety first! or perhaps
second?

2. Educational Foundations/Certification 17

CT/MRI. Nuclear medicine technologist. Radiologic
technologist (radiographer). Diagnostic medical sonographer.
How to prepare for a credentialing examination.

3. Work Sites 26

Small hospitals. Medium-sized hospitals. Large hospitals.
Outpatient imaging centers. Basic and applied research
settings. Educational institutions. Sales. Other work sites.

4. **Responsibilities and Opportunities
   for Advancement**..............................31
   Staff technologist. Chief technologist. Service director.
   Radiologist.

5. **People Skills, Managing Stress, and
   Avoiding Burnout** 35
   People skills. Your own stresses and strains. Burnout: how to
   recognize it. How to deal with stress and avoid burnout.

6. **Safety** 42
   Patient-related safety. Patient transferring and positioning.
   Contrast agents. Diseases and other disorders. You and the
   electromagnetic spectrum. Sonogram scanners. Radionuclide
   imaging. CT scan. MRI scans. Early effects of ionizing
   radiation (radiation sickness).

Bibliography......................................56
   Exam reviews and preparation. Technologists. Computed
   tomography. MRI. Sonography. Interventional and functional
   imaging. Nuclear medicine. Safety. Selected imaging
   periodicals.

Appendix A: Organization and Agency Acronyms 60

**Appendix B: Professional Organizations
and Addresses**.....................................61
   Accreditation. Registration/certification. Professional
   organizations—imaging. Other professional organizations.
   Canadian organizations.

**Appendix C: Accredited Nuclear Medicine
Technologist Programs** 76

**Appendix D: Accredited Radiologic Technologist
(Radiographer) Programs**..........................87

Appendix E: Accredited Diagnostic Medical Sonographer Programs. **131**

Appendix F: States that Require Licensure for Practice of Radiologic Technology **138**

Glossary **142**

ABOUT THE AUTHOR

Dr. Clifford J. Sherry is the CEO and a senior scientist and principal investigator with San Antonio Bio-Effects Research, LLC. He has spent the last thirty-five years in a variety of settings learning to identify problems and finding methods and procedures to solve them. He has been involved in the conception, preparation, execution, and presentation of basic and applied research. He has professional publications in more than twenty-five different referenced scientific journals. Much of this research has focused on how the nervous system processes information. In addition to his work in neurophysiology, Dr. Sherry also has worked and published in the areas of psychopharmacology, reproductive behavior/physiology, teratology, and the biobehavioral effects of electromagnetic fields and acoustics.

Dr. Sherry has taught human physiology and psychopharmacology, as well as perception and theories of learning, to more than two thousand students of widely varying backgrounds and abilities. He has presented his ideas to lay and professional audiences via public speeches, lectures, and workshops. He has an ever-increasing number of articles in magazines that focus on, but are not limited to, making science, medicine, computers, and the law understandable to nonspecialists. His books include *Contemporary World Issues: Endangered Species* and *Contemporary World Issues: Animal Rights,* both with ABC-CLIO, Santa Barbara, CA;

The New Science of Technical Analysis: Using the Statistical Techniques of Neuroscience to Uncover Order and Chaos in the Markets and *Mathematics of Technical Analysis: Applying Statistics to Trading Stocks, Options, and Futures,* both with Probus Publishing Co., Chicago; *Inhalants* and *Drugs and Eating Disorders,* both with Rosen Publishing Group, New York; and a previous edition of *Opportunities in Medical Imaging,* VGM Career Books, Lincolnwood, IL. He is currently at work on his next book, *The Incredible Secrets of Peppers,* for the Avery Publishing Group, New York.

FOREWORD

I believe that one of the most rewarding occupations is that of radiologic technologist, operating modern medical imaging equipment such as CT, MRI, nuclear medicine, ultrasound, and other scanners. I can remember, after having invented and built the first whole body CT scanner, convincing my first radiologic technologist to learn about CT and to run my machine. At first, he was hesitant about using such a new and previously unheard of device, but after a short time he became fascinated with my new instrument, and he made a career of not only using the machine, but of teaching other technologists about the use of CT scanners. His name was Charlie Seijo, and he's still in the field. That was almost twenty years ago, and during those two decades, this imaging revolution in medicine that I started has spread throughout the world.

Today each of many hundreds of thousands of scanners in use depends on the services of several knowledgeable and skilled radiologic technicians. Being able to run one of those machines is rewarding; viewing the images that you made with the machine is rewarding; knowing that your images can often pinpoint the medical diagnosis of the patient's ills, and frequently save the patient's life, is rewarding. In fact, just working at the high end of advanced technological development is in itself rewarding.

Being a radiologic technologist requires constant learning throughout your career. There are always new improvements to the scanners in this ever-evolving field, new medical diagnoses, and new methods for scanning patients. If you like doing things by rote, this is not the field for you; but if you enjoy learning about the new and latest in technology, if being at the forefront of medical developments excites you, then this *is* the field for you. Good luck and may you never have a dull moment!

Robert S. Ledley
Chairman, Computerized Medical Imaging Society
Professor, Georgetown University
Inductee, National Inventor's Hall of Fame

ACKNOWLEDGMENTS

I would like to thank my wife, Nancy, who helped edit and proof this book. Without her help and encouragement, this book could not have been written.

INTRODUCTION

A revolution is happening in medicine, and you can be part of it. Medical imaging began with the discovery of X rays by Wilhelm Konrad Roentgen on November 5, 1895, and it continues to this day. In fact, improvements to and refinements of existing imaging technologies and discovery of new technologies will undoubtedly continue well into the twenty-first century. These techniques will provide an ever clearer and more detailed window into the body and its functions.

These technologies include sonography, computed tomography, and magnetic resonance imaging, which have been in use for some time. They also include newer techniques, such as positron emission tomography and single-photon emission computerized tomography.

With appropriate training and experience, you can help shape the future of medical imaging. This book will provide the basic information that you will need to obtain this training and experience. The future is yours. Enjoy it!

CHAPTER 1

WHAT WOULD HAVE HAPPENED?

Wilhelm Conrad Röntgen (Roentgen) was born on March 27, 1845, in Lennep, in the lower Rhine Province in Germany. When he was three years old, his family moved to Apeldoorn in the Netherlands, where he attended the Institute of Martinus Herman van Doorn. He did not show any special aptitude, except perhaps for making mechanical contrivances. Röntgen entered a technical school at Utrecht, but was expelled (apparently unfairly) for drawing a caricature of one of his teachers. He entered the University of Utrecht in 1865 to study physics, but he did not have the credentials required for a regular student. When he heard that the Polytechnic at Zurich allowed students to enter by passing an examination, he took and passed the test and began studies in mechanical engineering. He attended lectures given by Rudolf Julius Emmanuel Clausius and August Adolph Eduard Kundt, who both exerted great influence on his professional development. Röntgen graduated with a Ph.D. from the University of Zurich in 1869, was appointed an assistant to Kundt, and then moved with him first to Wurzburg and then to Strasbourg. Röntgen's first published work dealing with the specific heat of gases was published in 1870, followed in a few years by a paper dealing with the thermal conductivity of crystals. In 1874, he qualified as a lecturer at Strasbourg University, was appointed to a professorship at the Academy of Agriculture at Hohenheim in Wurtemberg in 1875, and returned to Strasbourg as professor of physics in 1876. By 1879 he had moved to the chair of physics at the University of Giessen and returned to the University of Wurzburg in 1888, where he joined such notables as Hermann Ludwig Ferdinand von Helmholtz and Hendrik Antoon Lorentz. He moved to the University of Munich in 1900 and remained there for the rest of his life.

It was at Wurzburg where he made his famous discovery. Röntgen was working on experiments dealing with cathode rays, which occur when an electric current is passed through a gas at extremely low pressure. He was particularly interested in the luminescence that these rays set up in certain chemicals. On November 5, 1895, he was working in a darkened room and had enclosed the cathode ray tube in a thin cardboard tube. While working, he saw a flash of light that did not come from the tube. He looked up and noted that a paper coated with barium platinocyanide—one of the luminescent substances—some distance away, was glowing. The cathode rays, which were blocked by the cardboard tube, could not have reached the paper.

It is interesting to speculate. What would you have done if you had been in Röntgen's shoes? Would you have ignored the glowing paper and turned back to your original experiment? If so, then you would have missed the opportunity to make a major discovery. If Röntgen had turned back to his original experiment, would someone else have discovered and characterized these mysterious waves? Probably, perhaps even certainly. But, then, perhaps not. And even if they were discovered by someone else, when would the discovery have taken place? For example, when Sir William Crookes, the inventor of the cathode ray tube, heard of Röntgen's discovery, he realized that he had observed X ray before Röntgen, but did not know that he had.

Fortunately, Röntgen was a curious fellow; he turned the tube off and the paper darkened. He turned the tube back on again, and it glowed. He walked into the next room, turned the tube on, and noted that the paper glowed. At this point, he decided that some sort of radiation was coming from the cathode ray tube. This radiation was highly penetrating and invisible to the eye. It would pass through a considerable thickness of paper and even through thin pieces of metal. He had no idea about the nature of this form of radiation, so he called it an X ray, the name we still use today.

Röntgen knew he was on to something and wanted to publish his results before someone else beat him to it. But he also knew he needed more data. So, for the next seven weeks he experimented furiously. In one experiment, he had his wife hold her hand over a photographic plate while he exposed it to X rays. When he developed the plate he discovered an image of his wife's hand, which showed the shadows of the bones in her hand and the ring on her finger. The bones were surrounded by the penumbra of flesh, which was more permeable to the X rays and threw a fainter shadow. This was the first ever Röntgenogram, or X ray. He submitted his first paper on December 28, 1895, to the Wurzburg Physico-Medical Society, where he announced his discovery and reported on all of the fundamental properties of these waves. He was basically a shy man who preferred to work alone. He built most of the apparatuses he used in his experiments. According to popular folklore, when Röntgen was asked what he thought when he discovered X rays, he is said to have replied, "I did not think, I experimented."

If you have access to the Internet, you can read this paper at *http://www.emory.edu/X-RAYS/centuary_05.htm.* He called his paper, "On a New Kind of Ray, A Preliminary Communication." Röntgen sent copies of his paper and some X-ray photos to a number of renowned physicists on January 1, 1886. The news was spread by the popular media. The first story appeared in *Die Presse* on January 5, 1896, and in the *London Standard* on January 6, 1886. The X-ray phenomenon swept over Europe and America, and in the year following Röntgen's publication of his paper, almost one thousand scientific papers and as many as forty-nine books were published describing X rays.

The first public lecture on X rays was given by Röntgen on January 23, 1896. During this lecture, he called for a volunteer—Rudolf Albert von Kolliker, a Swiss anatomist and physiologist who was eighty years old at the time—and x-rayed his hand.

When X rays pass through tissue on the way to a photographic plate, they cast a shadow. Bones appear white on black. Metal objects also appear white. Within four days after the news of X rays reached the United States they were used to locate a bullet in the leg of a patient. It took a number of years to discover that X rays were potentially dangerous and could cause cancer and mutations.

Röntgen shared the Rumford Medal of the Royal Society with Phillipp Eduard Anton von Lenard, his mentor, in 1896. He received the first Nobel prize in physics in 1901 for his discovery of X rays. The unit of radiation exposure or intensity was named in his honor in 1928. It is called the Roentgen (R).

Röntgen never attempted to patent any aspect of X-ray production or to make any financial gain from his discovery. The inflationary period following World War I impoverished many Germans, including Röntgen. He died in relatively straitened circumstances in Munich on February 10, 1923, of a carcinoma of the intestine.

MOVING X RAYS

Thomas Edison began experimenting with X rays shortly after hearing about Röntgen's discovery. Edison had trouble obtaining X-ray tubes, so he made his own. Some of these early tubes were essentially modified electric light bulbs. Edison's work with X rays was wide ranging, but he focused most of his efforts improving the methods used for viewing X rays, where a screen coated with a fluorescent material replaced the photographic film. He reportedly tested more than eighteen hundred materials, finally settling on calcium tungstate. In March of 1896, Edison incorporated a screen coated with this material into the Vitascope. Renamed the fluoroscope, this device became the standard tool that physicians used to view X rays, particularly since it allowed movements of bones and organs.

In the late 1940s and early 1950s, virtually every shoe store that sold shoes to children had a shoe fitting X-ray unit. The dominant company in this area was the Adrain X-ray Company of Milwaukee, Wisconsin. The machine was designed by Brooks Stevens. It consisted of an X-ray tube mounted near the floor and a fluorescent screen. The X rays penetrated the shoes and feet and presented an image of the shoes and feet on the screen. Most of these machines had three ports: one for the customer, one for the customer's parent, and one for the salesperson. The dangers associated with these machines was recognized as early as 1950; they were effectively banned by thirty-three states by 1970 and strictly regulated in the remaining states.

IMPROVEMENTS

X-ray machines would have remained a laboratory curiosity, were it not for H. C. Snook and his invention of the interrupterless transformer (1907) and W. D. Coolidge of the General Electric Co. and his invention of the hot cathode X-ray tube (1913). Other developments, such as the use of cellulose nitrate film base (1916–18), soluble iodine compounds as contrast media (1919–21), and the Potter-Bucky grid, which increases image sharpness (1921), all helped move X rays out of the laboratory and into the hands of physicians.

By the 1930s virtually every hospital in the United States had some sort of X-ray equipment. Improvements such as xeroradiography and automatic film processing appeared in the 1950s.

Conventional X rays are essentially like photographs taken with a conventional camera, except that the operative agent is X rays, rather than light waves. They can provide an accurate picture of bones, but soft tissues in a structure such as the chest are all shown with approximately equal clarity.

COMPUTED TOMOGRAPHIC SCANNER:
A NEW APPROACH

Computed tomography (CT) or computer axial tomography (CAT) scanners work in the same manner, but the photographic plate that is used in conventional X rays is replaced by a detector whose output is connected to a computer. The process by which a CT scanner produces a cross-sectional image is quite complicated and requires a good deal of knowledge and understanding of physics, engineering, mathematics, and computer science. The computer uses a series of mathematical equations (algorithms) to use the output of the detector and the location of the patient to reconstruct the visual image that is transmitted to a television monitor, where it can be photographed for later examination.

Mr. Godfrey Hounsfield at the EMI Corporation (the people who recorded the Beatles!) began work on a CT scanner in 1968. The initial device was built at a laboratory in Hayes, England, and used an americium isotope as the source of γ-rays. Using simple phantoms (spheres, etc.), it took this device nine days to scan the object and two and a half hours to process a single image. The γ-ray source was replaced with an X-ray tube and this reduced the scan time to nine hours. For his work on the CT scanner, Hounsfield shared the 1979 Nobel prize in medicine with Dr. Allan M.

Cormack, who worked in South Africa in the physics department of the University of Cape Town and the Department of Radiology at the Groote Schuur Hospital, and who independently developed the algorithms associated with scanners.

The first prototype unit was prepared and installed for clinical studies of the brain in the Atkinson Morley Hospital near Wimbledon in 1972. The first three production units of a CT scanner, called the Mark I, were installed at the Mayo Clinic in Rochester, Massachusetts General Hospital in Boston, and Presbyterian-St.Lukes Hospital in Chicago. Mallinckrodt Institute of Radiology made history as the first institution to have two CT scanners. The Mark I was limited to scanning of the head because of the long scan time (four and a half minutes) and because it was necessary to eliminate any air gap between the scanner and the anatomical object. An air gap would attenuate the X-ray signal.

The Mark I utilized an X-ray beam that was collimated to a pencil beam and two detectors that were rigidly coupled by means of a yoke. The source-detector makes one sweep or translation across the patient, and the internal structures of the body attenuate the X-ray beam according to their density. The result is called a view. A total of 180 translations are performed, each separated by 1°.

The second generation scanner, called the EMI 5000, was made available in the summer of 1975. The 5000 series scanner could complete a scan in eighteen seconds. It produced the first images of the chest and abdomen. The 5000 series utilized a 10° fan beam and thirty detectors. The source-detector scanned across the patient and produced thirty views with 0.33° of angular difference between views obtained by neighboring detectors. The source-detector would then rotate 10° and repeat the process. This required only eighteen rotational movements.

General Electric, Siemens, Toshiba, Elscint, and Shimadzu also began marketing third generation scanners in 1975. In these scanners, the source-detector array pivoted around the patient in a single rotational movement. Depending on the manufacturer, the X-ray tube is either pulsed or on continuously. Typical scan times were two to four seconds.

Fourth generation scanners became available in the late 1970s. In these scanners the X-ray tube rotates, but the detector remains stationary. This requires more detectors, but because the X-ray tubes have very little inertial mass, very fast scan times are possible.

MAGNETIC RESONANCE IMAGING

The nuclei of hydrogen, phosphorus, sodium, potassium, and fluorine atoms spin on their axes, much like tiny subatomic tops. Carbon^{13}, which makes up about 1.1 percent of the carbon in the body, also spins in the same way. The movement of the positively charged protons (and neutrons that contain charged quarks) in the nuclei of these atoms produces magnetic fields. So, the spinning nuclei act as tiny magnets. In an applied magnetic field, these tiny atomic magnets tend to align in specific directions, usually in the same or opposite direction as the field. However, the alignment is never exact, and the nuclear magnets preceed (wobble) in the direction of the field, much like a spinning top wobbles in the earth's gravitational field. These nuclei resonate with the applied field.

If an applied magnetic field is oscillating at the same frequency with which the nuclei are precessing around the steady magnetic field, the nuclei all flip to one state or another (i.e., the same or opposite direction of the applied field). When the oscillating field is removed, the nuclei flip back to the original state. When this flip occurs, the nuclei release a small amount of energy. The nuclei become tiny radio transmitters. If a suitable coil (antenna) is present, it can detect this energy. Magnetic resonance can be used to code information about small units of tissue, and this information can then be used to create an image. By 1974, scientists had produced an NMR (nuclear magnetic resonance) proton image of a dead mouse. The first human in vivo (living tissue in a living body) NMR image was produced in 1977.

By applying a broad sweep of frequencies, George Radda and his colleagues in the Department of Biochemistry at Oxford and engineers at the Oxford Instruments Group and the Oxford Research Systems developed the surface coil in 1980. The surface coil consists of a few turns of wire about a centimeter in diameter. This coil influences the nuclei in a small volume of tissue, approximately the same area as the coil and as deep as the coil's radius. This allowed Radda and his colleagues to study the phosphorus spectra in different parts of an anesthetized rat. They chose phosphorus because it is part of the ATP (adenosine triphosphate) molecule; this molecule stores energy that is released during the metabolism of food until it is needed.

By 1982–83, Radda and his colleagues, using large superconducting magnets with a clear bore of twenty centimeters, could study the phosphorus spectra in vivo in the arm muscles of normal human volunteers. The muscles could be at rest, exercising, or recovering from exercise. Radda's group could distinguish the various forms of phosphate that were present. During the same time period, scientists also were studying phosphorus metabolism in human babies.

Dr. Robert Schulman and his colleagues at Yale University studied carbon[13] metabolism in vivo in humans. They utilized glucose labeled with carbon[13] to follow glucose metabolism in the liver.

Dr. Radda set up the first clinical MRI facility at the John Radcliffe Hospital in Oxford in 1983. They used a system built by Oxford Research Systems and studied the liver, brain, and heart, as well as other muscles. At about the same time, Dr. P. A. Bottomley's team developed the DRESS (Depth REsolved SpectroScopy). The problem with this technique is that it provides spatial information in only one dimension-depth below the surface.

In contrast to CT scanning, the MRI does not use ionizing radiation, but it does use very strong magnetic fields that may cause potential problems for individuals with (older) cardiac pacemakers or implanted ferromagnetic clips.

MRI presents anatomically correct images that can be used for localization, targeting, and navigation. MRI also can be used to study physiologic parameters such as diffusion, tissue perfusion, and flow, and these phenomena can be used to further define anatomical details. MRI can be used for guiding biopsies and tumor resection, where its greatest advantage over CT and fluoroscopy is that it does not expose the patient to ionizing radiation. In 1995, Gronemeyer and his colleagues performed the first interventional procedure in using an open MRI system. The GE 0.5 T Signa SP is an MRI system with a midfield intraoperative area. The system has a verticle gap between two vertically oriented magnets. The physician sits or stands in the gap and can perform percutaneous, interventional, endoscopic, and open surgical procedures. One of the most challenging aspects of interventional MRI is the development of nonmagnetic equipment and tools.

One of the key uses of interventional MRI is in guiding and imaging thermal surgery. Using focused ultrasound, surgeons can use MRI imaging to help restrict energy deposition to the target tissue and to signal the irreversible phase transition in the target tissue.

ULTRASONICS

Normal adult humans can hear sounds (pressure changes in the air) that range in frequency from 20 to 20,000 hertz (1 hertz = 1 cycle/sec.). Any frequency higher than 20,000 Hz is commonly called ultrasound. Bats and certain insects can produce and hear sounds as high as 120 kHz (k = kilo = 1000, therefore 120 kHz = 120,000 Hz).

The first man-made ultrasound did not appear until 1880, when Jacques and Pierre Curie demonstrated the piezoelectric effect at the Sorbonne in Paris. Pierre, who was twenty-one at the time of this discovery, was already an accomplished experimental and theoretical physicist. Eighteen years later, he would collaborate with his wife, Marie, in the discovery of radium. Röntgen also did some experiments with high frequency sound, but he stopped these experiments when he discovered X rays.

The piezoelectric effect occurs when certain crystals such as quartz, tourmaline, and Rochelle salt (sodium potassium tartrate), change the distribution of electric charge when they are subjected to mechanical stress. The first practical use of ultrasonics occurred during World War II, when SONAR (SOund Navigation And Ranging) was developed to detect submarines. The basic operating principal of SONAR is relatively straightforward. A beam of ultrasound is transmitted from the surface ship into the depths of the ocean. If this sound intersects a submarine (or other submerged object), a small amount of the ultrasound is reflected back to the surface and detected. The time required for the ultrasound to travel to the submarine and back to the surface is directly proportional to the distance between the submarine and the surface ship. Diagnostic ultrasound is based on these same principles.

MEDICAL ULTRASONIC IMAGING

The frequency of medical ultrasonic devices varies from 1 to 10 MHz (M = mega = 1,000,000, so 1 MHz = 1,000,000 Hz). The frequency and wavelength of sound, including ultrasound, are inversely proportional. That is, as frequency goes up, wavelength goes down. The ability to resolve small objects is directly related to wavelength. So, high frequency ultrasonics (10 MHz) allows better resolution than low frequency uultrasonics (1–2 MHz). Unfortunately, as frequency increases, so does absorption of ultrasonic sound, so high frequency ultrasound results in shallow penetration. Therefore, higher frequency ($\approx$ 10 MHz) ultrasonic transducers are used for small structures, such as the eye, while lower frequency ultrasonic transducers ($\approx$ 2.5 MHz) are used for abdominal examinations. Typically as frequency increases, its dispersion from the source decreases; that is, the beam becomes more collimated.

A transducer is a device that converts energy from one form to another. The transducer used in ultrasonic equipment converts electrical energy into sound energy and sound energy back into electrical energy. If a piezoelectric crystal is subjected to an electric signal that oscillates at a high frequency, the crystal will expand and contract at the same frequency. The crystal face acts much like the speaker cone in a high-fidelity speaker. The crystal face vibrates rapidly, which produces sound at the same frequency. These vibrations are coupled to the skin of the patient. Coupling gel or oil is used to eliminate air. When the ultrasound waves encounter any changes in the characteristic impedance within the body, such as might occur at the interface of two different tissues, echoes are reflected back to the piezoelectric transducer. These reflections—sounds—cause the crystal face to rapidly vibrate. The mechanical energy is converted into electric energy by the crystal. The crystals are very delicate. A 2.5 MHz crystal is only 0.31 millimeters thick.

The most common scan is called the B-scan (brightness mode), where the emitted pulses are scanned across a plane and the echoes are displayed in two dimensions.

It has been estimated that as many as 40 percent of all pregnant women in the United States have at least one B-scan ultrasound assessment. Since the fetus's head, trunk, and limbs are visualized, an obstetrician can determine if the fetus is suffering from abnormalities or growth retardation. Ultrasound examinations also can show if there is more than one fetus, as well as the sex of the fetus. Ultrasound images help an obstetrician guide a needle into the amniotic sac to withdraw fluid/cells that will show if the fetus has certain birth defects.

DOPPLER ULTRASONIC SCANNERS

Doppler ultrasonic scanners can be used to detect movement, such as blood flow. This technique depends on the fact that when the ultrasonic wave is reflected by a moving target, there is a Doppler shift in the frequency of the reflected waves. For example, if a 3 MHz wave is back scattered by blood flowing in the direction of the ultrasonic beam, and the blood is traveling at 1 meter/second, the Doppler shift will be about 4 kHz.

FUNCTIONAL IMAGING

In 1995, the world celebrated the centenary of Röntgen's discovery of X rays and how they could be used. Many improvements in medical imaging have occurred in that century. No one can predict the future of the next century, but it seems likely that basic scientists and their clinical colleagues will continue to seek new ways to look into the body as they try to unravel its mysteries. It also is likely that inventors, applied scientists, and technologists (engineers) will use these methods to develop new diagnostic tools.

In the twenty-first century, most of the breakthroughs will probably occur in functional or physiological imaging. One example of functional imaging is cardiac ultrasound, or echocardiography, which is now commonly used to show the movements of the heart walls and valves. Modern MRI scanners can acquire an image of a slice through the body in as little as 67 milliseconds, and the electron beam X-ray CT can acquire an image in 50 milliseconds. This allows scientists and clinicians to visualize the movement of the heart, the movement of the diaphragm, and the movement of the blood through tissues. If air is tagged with radio-dense gas, it can even show the distribution of a single breath.

However, perhaps the biggest breakthroughs will occur in imaging the brain. Using positron emission tomography (PET) and oxygen[15]=labeled water as a tracer, scientists have been able to determine, in normal volunteers, what parts of the brain are involved with speech and language. The PET scanner is used to determine changes in regional blood flow in the brain. It is assumed that when blood flow to a specific brain structure increases, it means the structure is involved in a specific task. Single photon emission computerized tomography allows scientists to detect regional changes in glucose metabolism. It is important to remember that these techniques provide a "snapshot" of complex, dynamic, continuous processes. It is possible that radioactively labeled neurotransmitters can potentially be identified using PET scans.

Changes in technology are occurring at a very rapid rate. As mentioned earlier, the first CT scanner, in 1968, took 9 days to scan a relatively simple phantom and 2.5 hours to produce an image. By the late 1970s, a scan could be accomplished in 1.6 seconds!

Developing new technology and/or improving existing technology is very costly. Many hospitals and freestanding imaging centers have one or more CT scanners and MRI scanners. It is likely that if PET scanners are demonstrated to be clinically useful, these centers will acquire them as well.

In 1985, MRI systems cost $750,000 to $1,900,000. It is currently estimated that the useful life of an MRI scanner is five to seven years. But, it is possible, even likely, that during that time period one or more major breakthroughs might occur. Should a center with an MRI scanner that still has several years of useful life be allowed to acquire a new device? Concerns about the constantly increasing costs of medical care have transformed this from an economic question (Can we afford to buy one?) to a political question (Should we allow them to buy one?). For example, Section 1122 of the Social Security Act (see Public Law 92-603) requires prior approval by local and state planning agencies for any capital expenditures of more than $100,000 for any institution that receives federal funds via Medicare, Medicaid, maternal and child health legislation, and/or federal employee insurance programs.

SAFETY FIRST! OR PERHAPS, SECOND?

Thomas Edison, William J. Morton, and Nikola Tesla were among the first to suggest that X rays and fluorescent substances might be dangerous. Edison, a prolific inventor, might have gone on to invent other X-ray related devices, but for one incident. An assistant and longtime friend, Clarence Dally, received a serious X-ray burn. The burn was severe enough to cause the amputation of both arms and, ultimately, his death in 1904. Dally is generally counted as the first X-ray fatality in the United States. The American physicist, Elihu Thomson, exposed the little finger of his left hand to an X-ray tube for several days for a half an hour a day. This caused pain, swelling, stiffness, erythema, and blistering. This convinced Thomson and others that X rays were potentially dangerous. Dr. William Herbert Rollins, a Boston dentist, demonstrated that X rays could kill adult guinea pigs and the fetus of a pregnant guinea pig. Between 1896 and 1904, Dr. Rollins developed a number of devices designed to minimize the risk of X-ray burns. These devices included a collimator, which was designed to restrict the X-ray beam by a diaphragm and leaded tube housings.

He also was instrumental in developing high voltage tubes to limit patient dose and to improve the diagnostic quality of X rays by inserting a leather or aluminum filter (filtration).

Rome Vernon Wagner, an X-ray tube manufacturer, proposed that people who might be exposed to X rays should carry a photographic plate in their pocket. The plate would be developed each day to determine if exposure to X rays had occurred. This is the forerunner of the film badge that is commonly used today.

The British Roentgen Society, formed in 1915, and the American Roentgen Ray Society, formed in 1922, began to provide radiation protection recommendations.

CHAPTER 2

EDUCATIONAL FOUNDATIONS/ CERTIFICATION

If you are considering a career in medical imaging, it is a good idea to visit an imaging center in a hospital or clinic and talk to several of the professionals who are employed there. They can provide you with insights and information about the field of medical imaging. Try and attend the annual convention of either the American Society of Radiologic Technologists (ASRT), the technologist section of the Society of Nuclear Medicine (SNM), or the Society of Diagnostic Medical Sonographers. You can find the location and time of the meeting by writing to them. Their addresses can be found in Appendix B. It is possible that these organizations have a local chapter that meets near you. If so, try and find out when and where and plan to attend some meetings.

The place to begin planning a career in medical imaging is in high school. The secondary school curriculum is generally divided into units, where a unit is equal to one year's work in a single subject. It is assumed that a high school graduate will have completed sixteen to twenty units of high school work. A typical high school curriculum that would prepare a student for a career in medical imaging should include 1 unit each in biology, chemistry, and physics; 2 to 3 units in mathematics; 2 units in social studies, including psychology, if possible; and 4 units of English. Because the United States is becoming more culturally diverse with each passing year, 3 to 4 units of foreign language will help the student understand members of other cultures. Electives (4 to 8 units) should include a course in computer science, if available, as well as additional courses in science and mathematics.

It is a good idea to check with a guidance counselor or advisor to determine the general entrance requirements for professional training programs that you may be interested in. It is best to pursue a program that is accredited by the Committee of Allied Health Education and Accreditation (CAHEA) of the American Medical Association (AMA). Currently accredited programs for nuclear medicine technologists, radiologic technologists, and sonographers are shown in Appendices C, D, and E, respectively. It is important to note that new programs constantly are added and old programs deleted from this list. So, it is best to check the current edition of the *Allied Health Education Directory,* which is published annually by the CAHEA. Additional information can be obtained from the professional or registration/certification organizations listed in Appendix B.

CT/MRI

There are currently no license, certification, or registration requirements necessary to work as a CT or MRI technologist. However, many technologists hold certifications or registrations in other paramedical fields, such as medical technology or nursing and especially radiologic technology (radiographer). The credentialing agency is the American Registry of Radiologic Technologists (ARRT). The ARRT provides advanced-level examinations in computed tomography and magnetic resonance imaging. The licensing laws covering the practice of these professions vary from state to state. A current list of states that require licensure for radiologic technologists is shown in Appendix F. The rules and regulations for licensure change from time to time, so it is best to check with the state board of health. The state also might have a radiologic safety board or similar program that regulates professionals in radiology and related professions.

NUCLEAR MEDICINE TECHNOLOGIST

The applicant for admission into a professional training program must have graduated from high school (or its equivalent). Postsecondary competencies in mathematics and science courses such as human anatomy and physiology, physics, and chemistry, as well as specialized classes in medical terminology and medical ethics, are important. Oral and written communication skills also are emphasized.

The professional portion of the program is one year in length and leads to a certificate. However, the professional training can be integrated into a two-year program leading to an associate degree or a four-year program leading to a baccalaureate degree. The curriculum for an accredited program will have classes in patient care, nuclear physics, instrumentation and statistics, health physics, biochemistry, immunology, radiopharmacology, administration, radiation biology, clinical nuclear medicine, radionuclide therapy, and an introduction to computer application.

Upon satisfactory completion of the training program, the applicant can sit for the credentialing examination offered by the Nuclear Medicine Technology Certification Board (NMTCB) or the American Registry of Radiologic Technologist (ARRT). The NMTCB examination is a timed test (one hour and forty-five minutes) consisting of ninety questions. The examination is given on a computer, and the computer will not allow you to move on to the next question without answering the current question on the screen. The examination is based on the number of questions answered correctly, so there is no penalty for guessing. The examination is task-oriented and deals with the application of basic knowledge to nuclear medical technology practice. Sample examination questions can be found at their web site (*http://www.nmtcb.org*). Calculators are allowed if they are noiseless and battery or solar powered. If you successfully pass the examination, you are granted the right to use the title Certified Nuclear Medicine Technologist and the initials CNMT after your name. Your name will be listed in the *NMTCB Directory of Certified Nuclear Medicine Technologists.* You are required to renew your certification each year.

The ARRT exam consists of 200 questions in five areas: radiation protection (22 questions), radiopharmaceutical preparation (22), intrumental quality control (28), diagnostic procedures (114), and patient care (14). Individuals with a baccalaureate or associate degree in one of the biological or physical sciences and national certification as a registered medical technologist, registered radiologic technologist, or registered nurse also may request to sit for the certification examination. They must have completed either 6,000 hours (if experience began before January 1, 1979) or 8,000 hours (after January 1, 1979) of clinical experience in nuclear medicine technology under the supervision of a physician (M.D./D.O.) board certified in nuclear radiology (ABR), nuclear medicine (ABNM), or isotopic pathology (ABP).

RADIOLOGIC TECHNOLOGIST (RADIOGRAPHER)

The applicant for admission for professional training as a radiographer must be a high school graduate (or equivalent), and the high school curriculum described above also would be appropriate. The typical program is either two or four years in length and is integrated into an associate or baccalaureate degree plan.

The typical curriculum at a CAHEA-accredited institution would include introduction to radiography, radiographic procedures, principles of radiographic exposure, imaging equipment, film processing, evaluation of radiographs, radiation physics, principles of radiation protection and radiation biology, and radiographic pathology. It also should include courses on human anatomy and physiology, medical ethics and law, medical terminology, methods of patient care, quality assurance, and computer literacy. A plan for a well-structured, competency-based clinical education, where the student interacts with patients under the supervision of a physician or technologist, is also an important part of the curriculum.

Upon satisfactory completion of the training program, the applicant can sit for the credentialing examination offered by the ARRT. However, candidates for registration must have good moral character. Anyone convicted of a felony or any offense involving moral turpitude will not be permitted to sit for the examination until they have served their entire sentence (including probation and parole) and have had their civil rights restored.

ARRT currently administers eight examinations, three in the primary radiological sciences: radiography, nuclear medicine technology (described above), and radiation therapy technology; as well as five advanced-level examinations: cardiovascular-interventional technology, mammography, computer tomography, magnetic resonance imaging, and quality management.

The radiography examination consists of 200 questions in the following areas: radiation protection (30 questions), equipment operation and maintenance (30), image production and evaluation (50), radiographic procedures (60), and patient care (30). Upon satisfactory completion of an accredited training program and passing of the certification examination, the technologist will receive a certificate and pocket credential and have the right to use the title, Registered Radiographer. The certificate must be renewed annually. In addition, the technologist has the right to use the abbreviation R. T. (ARRT) in connection with his or her name on documents, business cards, and name tags. The technologist's name also will appear in the *American Registry of Radiologic Technologists,* which is published every other year.

The radiation therapy exam consists of 200 questions: 40 questions dealing with radiation protection and quality assurance, 130 questions dealing with treatment planning and delivery, and 30 questions dealing with patient care, management, and education. The radiation therapy technologist's work centers on utilizing radiation-producing equipment to administer therapeutic doses of radiation to patients, rather than utilizing this equipment for imaging.

DIAGNOSTIC MEDICAL SONOGRAPHER

Students seeking professional training as sonographers must be high school graduates (or equivalent), and the high school curriculum described above would be appropriate. Professional training programs are either two or four years in length and yield an associate or baccalaureate degree. Some individuals in four-year programs obtain a degree in radiology, with a minor in sonography. The typical curriculum at a CAHEA-accredited institution would include physical sciences, applied biological sciences, patient care, clinical medicine, applications of ultrasound, instrumentation, related diagnostic procedures, and image evaluation.

In order to sit for the credentialing examination offered by the American Registry of Diagnostic Medical Sonographers (ARDMS), graduates of these programs must have at least one year (35 hours/week for 48 weeks/year) of ultrasound/vascular clinical experience. Graduates of other two-year allied health training programs that focus on patient care, such as radiologic technology, respiratory therapy, occupational therapy, physical therapy, and registered nursing, may sit for the credentialing examination if they have one year of ultrasound/vascular clinical experience. Physicians (M.D. or D.O.) who are duly licensed to practice medicine in the United States may sit for the examination if they have one year of clinical experience in ultrasound/vascular. Graduates of two-year nonsonography programs are required to have twenty-four months of clinical experience in order to sit for the examination. ARDMS also allows individuals who were trained on the job to sit for the examination. They must have twenty-four months of clinical experience in ultrasound and an addition twenty-four months of training/experience in an allied health field, such as electrocardiographic or electroencephalo-graphic technology, licensed practical nurse, noninvasive testing, etc.

ARDMS offers four credentials: the registered diagnostic medical sonographer, the registered diagnostic cardiac sonographer, the registered vascular technologist, and the registered ophthalmic ultrasound biometrist. The candidate for registered diagnostic medical sonographer must pass the ultrasound physics and instrumentation examination and a specialty examination in obstetrics and gynecology, abdomen, neurosonology, or ophthalmology. The diagnostic cardiac sonographer must pass the cardiovascular principles and instrumentation and physics examinations and either the pediatric or adult echocardiography specialty examination. In order to become a registered vascular technologist, the candidate must pass the vascular physical principles and instrumentation examination, as well as the vascular technology examination. The candidate for registered ophthalmic ultrasound biometrist must pass the ophthalmic biometry examination in order to become registered.

The physics/principles examinations contain 120 multiple choice questions and cover the following subjects: elementary principles, propagation of ultrasound through tissues, ultrasound transducers, pulse echo instruments, principles of pulse echo imaging, images, storage and display, Doppler, image features and artifacts, quality assurance of ultrasound instruments, and bioeffects and safety. The speciality examinations contain 180 multiple choice questions and cover a variety of topics. For example, the obstetrics and gynecology speciality examination covers obstetrics (such as first trimester anatomy, second and third trimester anatomy, the placenta, assessment of gestational age, complications, amniotic fluid, genetic studies, fetal demise, fetal abnormalities, and coexisting disorders), gynecology (normal pelvic anatomy, reproductive physiology, infertility/endocrinology, postmenopausal anatomy and physiology, pelvic pathology, and extra-pelvic pathology), and patient care and preparation.

Upon successful completion of the education requirements and passing the examination, ARDMS provides a certificate, identification card, and lapel pin, as well as a listing in the *ARDMS Directory*. ARDMS also publishes a quarterly newsletter, *Registry Reports*.

HOW TO PREPARE FOR
A CREDENTIALING EXAMINATION

The first step in preparing for the credentialing examinations offered by NMTCB, ARRT, or ARDMS is to understand the appropriate eligibility requirements and be sure that you have met them. Make sure that the application and supporting paperwork (transcripts, diplomas, etc.) are turned in well before the application deadline. It is important to know the date and time of the examination, as well as the site of the examination, and to be sure that you know how to find the examination site.

Read over the application packet so you know what can be brought into the examination room. Generally this is limited to several sharpened soft lead pencils (#2), with erasers. Battery powered calculators are commonly allowed, but sharing calculators is not. As these tests are timed, it is a good idea to have a wristwatch, so you can pace yourself. Typically you will not be allowed to bring papers, books, dictionaries, or any other material into the examination room. Scratch work is done in the margins of the examination itself.

The tests are scored on the basis of number of correct answers, so if you do not know an answer, guess! But, make a mark in the margin of the examination and come back to that question if time permits. Each of the credentialing organizations have different methods for attempting to equate the difficulty level of each version of the examination (i.e., new versions are used each time the examination is given) and the ability level of the group tested. The procedures are outlined in the application package of each organization.

These examinations are not meant to test basic knowledge, but rather the application of that knowledge to the practice of the profession. Be sure to read over the application package carefully and note what sort of questions are asked in the sample tests, as well as the distribution of questions in specific content areas. Also, be sure to take the practice test. Practice does improve performance.

In the weeks before the examination, review a current textbook in the appropriate area. It is also a good idea to review continuing education articles and teaching editorials in recent journals to provide a review of current clinical practice.

During the week(s) before the examination, be sure to get plenty of rest and eat well—no junk food! Get a good night's sleep the night before the examination.

On the day of the examination, arrive a few minutes early, sit down, close your eyes, and take a few slow, deep breaths. This will help you to relax. If you feel yourself getting nervous during the exam, take a minute to repeat this process. And be sure to keep your eyes on you own exam!

CHAPTER 3

WORK SITES

Medical imaging takes place in a variety of different settings. Because of the cost and size of CT and MRI scanners, this type of imaging tends to occur in hospitals and freestanding imaging centers. A recent poll provides detailed information about the work sites of nuclear medical technologists. It is likely that radiologic technologists work in essentially the same settings, although they may be more involved with imaging using more traditional X-ray equipment.

Sonography also occurs in these settings, but it is increasingly likely to find sonographic equipment and sonographers in the larger group medical practices, particularly those that deal with obstetrics and gynecology or ophthalmology, as well as those that deal with the cardiovascular system. It is also likely to find sonography equipment in outpatient clinics, health maintenance organizations, and state or county health departments.

SMALL HOSPITALS

About 5 percent of all nuclear medical technologists work in small hospitals (hospitals with fewer than one hundred beds). These hospitals are found in small cities and rural communities.

While they may have traditional X-ray equipment, it is very unlikely that they would have a CT or, especially, an MRI scanner. If the hospital has an obstetrics/gynecology department, it is likely that it will be supplied with sonography equipment.

MEDIUM-SIZED HOSPITALS

About a third of all nuclear medical technologists work in medium-sized hospitals (one hundred to three hundred beds). Such a hospital is likely to have a variety of imaging equipment, including traditional X-ray equipment, a CT scanner, and MRI scanner. It is likely that the imaging department will have several sonography machines, and it is possible that the obstetrics/gynecology department may have its own sonography equipment and dedicated sonographers.

LARGE HOSPITALS

About half of all nuclear medicine technologists work in large hospitals (more than three hundred beds). Large hospitals, especially large teaching hospitals that are associated with medical schools, are likely to have an X-ray or radiology department, as well as a medical imaging department that has one or more CT scanners, an MRI scanner, and possibly a PET or SPECT scanner. Sonography services may be provided by a separate sonography department, or they may be part of the radiology or imaging department. Increasingly obstetrics/gynecology, ophthalmology, and cardiac care services have their own dedicated sonography equipment and sonographers.

OUTPATIENT IMAGING CENTERS

The cost of CT and MRI scanners is prohibitive. Improvements in technology occur more rapidly than the useful life cycle of existing equipment. Some health care planners believe that outpatient imaging centers may provide the most economical method of providing CT and MRI services. One outpatient imaging center can serve patients from a number of hospitals, health maintenance organizations, and individual physicians. Currently about 8.5 percent of all nuclear medicine technologists work in this setting.

BASIC AND APPLIED RESEARCH SETTINGS

Basic and applied researchers use imaging as a tool to help them understand how the body works. They also want to use imaging equipment to determine how disease and other pathological processes affect the body.

For example, the 1990s have been declared the "decade of the brain." It is hoped that as we enter the twenty-first century we will begin to understand how our brains work. Imaging and medical imagers will be at the forefront of this work. Neuroscientists believe that MRI and PET scanners may act as "windows" on the mind. These scientists and their clinical colleagues (neurologists, neurosurgeons) hope that these imaging devices will help them make a functional map of the brain. PET scanners, for example, can track brain function. In a typical experiment, a female volunteer might be injected with radioactive glucose, the sugar the brain uses as its fuel. The more active a part of the brain is, the more glucose it uses. So, if the volunteer were asked to do a simple math problem, one part of the brain would light up. If she were asked, "Who was the first president of the United States?" a different part would light up. Neuroscientists using a PET scanner recently discovered that the part of the brain that learns and remembers human faces is entirely different from the part of the brain that learns and recalls man-made objects. Current PET scanners cannot resolve structures less than half an inch apart. Considering your brain is not much larger than your two fists held together, half an inch can contain a variety of different structures. So, current PET scanners allow scientists to obtain a relatively crude functional map. But before PET scanners, the functional map was even cruder! SPECT, a close relative of PET, can monitor blood flow in the brain. Blood flow is another sign of activity. The more active a particular brain structure is, the more blood it receives. MRI scanners cannot detect brain function, but they can provide an accurate map of the brain because they can resolve structures that are only 0.05 inches apart.

Sonography is also used in research. For example, veterinarians are using sonography to determine the fat content of beef "on the hoof," that is, while the steer is still alive.

EDUCATIONAL INSTITUTIONS

Many of the teachers in CAHEA-accredited programs for nuclear medicine technology, radiologic technology, and sonography are themselves technologists. About 3 percent of all nuclear medicine technologists describe themselves as educators. As shown in Appendices C through E, these educational programs are found in a variety of institutions, including hospitals, two-year junior or community colleges, and four-year colleges and universities, as well as a number of technical schools.

SALES

About 2.5 percent of technologists are employed as salespersons, selling equipment, radiopharmaceuticals, and other supplies. In contrast to technologists who actually do imaging, salespersons must generally be willing to travel. Depending on the size of their territory, salespersons may be away from home for as long as several weeks at a time. Salespersons are often called on to train physicians and staff on how to use the equipment or products that they sell, demonstrate the equipment or products at medical conferences and trade shows, and troubleshoot equipment when it malfunctions.

Salespersons must be fairly aggressive and possess excellent communication skills. They also must be willing to work independently and thus must be self-starters. Technical sales is potentially a very lucrative career for a technologist.

OTHER WORK SITES

Certified nuclear medicine and radiologic technologists receive a good deal of training on radiation safety. Therefore, they can act as radiation health and safety personnel for federal, state, county, or local health and radiation control agencies, as well as industries whose personnel could potentially be exposed to ionizing radiation (e.g., nuclear power plants).

CHAPTER 4

RESPONSIBILITIES AND OPPORTUNITIES FOR ADVANCEMENT

It is important to note that only a physician, either an M.D. or a D.O., can order traditional radiologic examinations, as well as CT, MRI, PET, or sonogram scans. Furthermore, only a physician can interpret the results of such a scan. Doctors of chiropractic and podiatry can order and interpret traditional radiologic examinations.

STAFF TECHNOLOGIST

This is the entry-level position. Staff technologists are the people who work "in the trenches" and have day-to-day contact with patients. Therefore, it is vital that technologists should be compassionate people, who demonstrate in their interactions with patients, that they care about their feelings and concerns. One way to show this is to spend a few minutes with each patient to be sure that the patient understands the procedure. During this time, a technologist also can alleviate the patient's fears about the procedure. At all times technologists should exhibit a professional demeanor. By their actions and speech, they create the impression of professional competence. Technologists acquire an adequate knowledge and understanding of each patient's medical history so that they can perform the ordered diagnostic procedure and maximize its interpretability for the physician who ordered it. Technologists are responsible for instructing the patient before and during the procedure and helping to position the patient. They are also responsible for determining whether the procedure was carried out correctly. If the patient moves, or if the equipment is not working properly and the scan is uninterpretable, the scan should be repeated, so as to save the patient the time and trouble of having to return to the imaging center for a new scan. Technologists must use their knowledge of radiation physics and safety regulations to minimize radiation exposure to their patients and themselves. In addition, while the patient is under the technologist's care, the technologist must be able to recognize emergency conditions and be able to initiate emergency lifesaving first aid when appropriate.

About half of the nuclear medicine technologists at this level indicate that imaging is their main job responsibility. In addition to their duties involving imaging, these technologists must also be able to prepare and administer radiopharmaceuticals. They must be able to use appropriate laboratory equipment to quantify the amount and distribution of radionucleotides in the patient and in specimens obtained from the patient (e.g., urine or stools). Technologists must be prepared to monitor the quality of all procedures and products in the laboratory.

Radiologic technologists have similar duties. In addition to specialized scans, such as CT or MRI, these technicians are likely to be involved with using more traditional X-ray equipment. They must be able to use their knowledge of anatomy, physiology, and radiographic technique to correctly instruct the patient about the tests and procedures they perform. These technologists also help position the patients. They are responsible for processing film and evaluating radiologic equipment.

Sonographers, because of the nature of the sonographic technique, often have more contact with the patient. Sonography equipment is a bit less intimidating than the equipment used in CT or MRI scans, so patients might be a bit less overwhelmed. Sonographers must be able to perform sonography scans and record anatomical, pathological, and physiological data that will help the physician interpret the results of the scan.

CHIEF TECHNOLOGIST

The chief technologist, whether he or she is a nuclear medicine or radiologic technologist or a sonographer, supervises staff technologists, students acquiring clinical experience as part of their certification process, laboratory assistants, and other laboratory personnel. Since the chief technologist has more experience, this individual also helps the staff technologists with difficult scans.

SERVICE DIRECTOR

The service director supervises the chief technologist and other personnel. This person works in concert with the medical staff and hospital administrators to identify and procure new equipment. He or she also participates in routine quality control, documenting laboratory operations and helping with any departmental inspections conducted by various licensing, regulatory, and accrediting agencies. The director is also responsible for ordering and maintaining supplies and for scheduling patient examinations.

RADIOLOGIST

The medical director of an imaging department is likely to be a radiologist or a physiatrist. A radiologist is a physician who has specialized training in the diagnostic and therapeutic use of X rays and other forms of radiant energy. A physiatrist is a physician who specializes in physical medicine and uses heat, electricity, and ionizing radiation in the diagnosis and treatment of disease.

CHAPTER 5

PEOPLE SKILLS, MANAGING STRESS, AND AVOIDING BURNOUT

With the possible exception of a woman who comes to have a routine sonogram during pregnancy, almost everyone (which includes family members) who comes to an imaging center is under a good deal of stress. Such people may not be on their best behavior.

The reason that they have come to the imaging center is because someone, usually their family physician or some medical specialist, suspects (or knows) that they have a serious, potentially life-threatening, medical condition.

The patient may have just heard frightening words such as *cancer, heart disease, stroke,* or *internal bleeding.* Or the patient may be an accident victim or the victim of a violent crime, such as a shooting or a stabbing. Victims will probably still be shaken by whatever incident brought them to the imaging center.

The patient may also be concerned about the cost of the scan. While the physician may consider the results of the scan vital to his or her ability to make a diagnosis and prescribe a treatment, the cost may not be a trivial consideration to the patient. Even with some types of insurance, the patient will probably pay 10 percent to 40 percent of the cost of the scan. A patient without insurance will have to bear the entire cost.

The equipment in the imaging center can be frightening. This is especially true of CT and MRI equipment that is large relative to the size of the patient and requires the patient to *enter* the machine and remain inside and very still for some time. The patient may also feel abandoned because the technologist and family members must leave the immediate area while the scan is being conducted. Infants, young children, and elderly people are more likely to be frightened by the imaging device than young or middle-aged adults. Sonographic equipment is smaller, and for most scans the technologist remains with the patient and actually manipulates the transducer to perform the scan. So, sonographic procedures might be somewhat less frightening.

Medical imaging is a highly technical field, and an imager will learn the technical side of the profession, such as how to do a CT scan and recognize a good image, at a CAHEA-approved school. But there is more to medical imaging than the technical side of things.

The technologist must always remember that what is being imaged is a person. Therefore, in addition to technical skills, the technologist must possess good people skills, as well as good communication skills. The technologist should be compassionate and have empathy for the patients that he or she works with and be able to communicate these feelings to the patient.

PEOPLE SKILLS

It is never too early to acquire people skills. The way to acquire people skills is to be around people, as big a cross section of different types of people as you can find, and interact with them. The process can begin in high school. Take part in extracurricular activities, such as clubs, teams, the band, or whatever interests you. Volunteer at a hospital, nursing home, homeless shelter, liter-

acy center, or crisis hot line. These organizations are always looking for volunteers, and volunteering will bring you into contact
with a wide variety of different types of people undergoing a variety of different stresses.

Another way to increase your people skills is by taking classes
in the social sciences. Choose this type of class when you have the
opportunity to choose electives. Classes dealing with psychology
or sociology are especially useful. Foreign languages are also
helpful; besides the language, you will acquire some insight into
the culture of the people who speak the language.

If you pursue a CAHEA-approved program that leads to an
associate or baccalaureate degree, you will probably have electives
in these programs, and you can select psychology or sociology
courses. You also can continue extracurricular activities and volunteer work. Be sure that these activities do not affect your course
work or grades.

Most school and public libraries have dozens of books dealing
with psychology, sociology, and self-help. The librarian or one of
your counselors should be able to help you locate appropriate
books. Bookstores also have dozens of hardback and paperback
books dealing with psychology, sociology, and self-help. Two self-
help books that might be especially helpful are *Coping with Difficult People* by Robert M. Bramson and *When Bad Things Happen
to Good People* by Harold S. Kushner. You can also get a good
deal of insight from books written by patients about their experiences. Your librarian or bookstore manager should be able to help
you locate books dealing with these topics.

YOUR OWN STRESSES AND STRAINS

People in the helping professions often have to deal with a good
deal of unrelieved stress in the workplace. These people include

doctors, nurses, imaging technologists, and other medical or allied medical professionals, as well as any other individuals, such as policemen and firemen, who work long and often irregular hours and come into contact with people who are under stress.

Members of these professions tend to do shift work. That is, they may work nine to five one week, and then from midnight to eight in the morning the next week. If there are not enough personnel to cover every shift, some technologists might be asked to work more than one shift. Or they may work between eighteen and twenty-four hours on the weekend and then be off for several days.

Members of these professions may also be on call, that is, they must be available to come into work on a moment's notice, in case of an emergency. If the number of technologists at a particular location is small, it may not be possible to rotate on-call duties.

BURNOUT: HOW TO RECOGNIZE IT

Burnout can be defined as a debilitating psychological condition brought on by unrelieved stress in the workplace. Although most people who study burnout look at stress in the workplace, students with unresolved stress can also suffer from burnout. This is especially true of students who must also work and potentially deal with family issues such as conflict with spouses or children.

The symptoms of burnout are relatively easy to recognize, especially in someone else! Generally the first symptom to appear is a depletion of energy reserves. This is characterized by chronic fatigue. You just feel tired all of the time. If you have poor eating habits, such as skipping meals or eating junk food or fast food, or if you have a poor sleep-wakefulness cycle, these effects can be magnified. If you are on call or if you do shift work, your sleep-wakefulness cycle is likely to be disrupted.

These factors often lead to the second symptom, lowered resistance to illness. When you reach this stage, you find that you have a lot of minor illnesses, such as colds and sore throats. Nothing life threatening, but debilitating nonetheless.

Individuals who are tired all of the time and mildly sick most of the time begin to recognize that something is wrong. At this stage you will probably experience dissatisfaction and pessimism about your work. If unresolved, this generally leads to an increase in absenteeism and inefficiency, which can be a real problem if you are working in a medical setting. If you make a mistake, you can hurt your patient or even yourself.

HOW TO DEAL WITH STRESS AND AVOID BURNOUT

The first step to avoid burnout is to be aware that it exists and that it is quite common for people in the helping professions. The second step is to learn what stress is and what being under stress can do to you. An excellent introduction to stress and the problems that it can cause is *Stress without Distress* by the late Dr. Hans Selye, the father of stress research.

The next step is to understand the nature of the stress that you are routinely confronted with. One good way to do this is to get a solid idea of what things bother you. Keep a notebook in your pocket, and each time you complain about your job (or your school) or your life, write down the complaint. Also keep your ears open. What do your colleagues complain about?

Listen to your body. Are you tired all the time? Do you feel tense? Are your muscles tight and sore? Do you grind your teeth? Have stomachaches? Headaches? Poor appetite? Write these things down in your notebook as well.

It is important to realize that stress exists and that it is probably not possible to avoid it completely. What you need to do is learn to manage stress. Do not let yourself become a workaholic! Although it might be difficult to do so, you should commit to changing gears. That means developing interests or hobbies that have nothing to do with your work (or your school activities, if you are a student). And spend time engaged in those non-job-related activities. But be sure that you pick something that you really enjoy. It is probably best to avoid competitive activities. For example, if you decide that you want to play golf, and you want to be the world's best golfer, and you are like 99 percent of the population, you will not have the innate talent to be the world's best. But if that is your goal, then your non-job activity might be as stressful as your job-related activities. So, pick something that you like and will not add to your level of stress.

Exercise is an important component of stress management. It can be something as simple as a brisk walk or even a not-so-brisk stroll. Or it can be a complete aerobic workout. But whatever it is, be sure to do it regularly.

Eat well! Note this does not mean a lot; it means eat well. Avoid junk food—things like chips, candy, and cookies. Also, avoid fast foods. They generally contain a lot of processed sugar, cholesterol, sodium, and other things you should avoid. And they generally do not contain an adequate amount of vitamins, minerals, and other essential nutrients. An occasional hamburger, fries, and milk shake are all right, but do not allow them to become your standard fare. Do not skip breakfast. When you eat, do not eat at your desk. Leave your work area and all of its problems. Sit down and eat, and try not to think about work. Do not talk about work or your workmates. Eat slowly and enjoy your food.

Learn to relax! If you cannot do anything else, learning to relax is probably the most important way to deal with stress and avoid burnout. There are a variety of ways to learn to relax. One simple way is to find a quiet place where you will not be disturbed. Sit down in a comfortable chair. Do not lie down, as it is likely that if you lie down and relax, you will fall asleep. Loosen tight clothing, take off your shoes, and remove any heavy jewelry. Close your eyes and take a few deep breaths. Then begin to breathe slowly and deeply. Relax your forehead and scalp. Let all of the wrinkles of your forehead relax and smooth out. Then relax the muscles of your face. Let your jaw muscles relax. Then your neck muscles. Let the relaxation flow to your shoulders, upper arms, lower arms, and hands. Continue to breathe slowly and deeply. Then relax the muscles of your trunk, and allow the relaxation to flow down your abdomen to your legs. Allow it to flow down your legs to your ankles, to the tips of your toes. Try not to fall asleep. Remain in this relaxed state for ten to fifteen minutes.

CHAPTER 6

SAFETY

PATIENT-RELATED SAFETY

When a patient is delivered to the imaging center, his or her immediate care is the responsibility of the staff of the center. While you are performing an imaging procedure, the patient's immediate care is your responsibility. Therefore, it is vital that you know enough about the patient's condition so that you know what to expect. But also be prepared for the unexpected! You must know what to do if a patient stops breathing, has a convulsion, or has some other minor or major difficulty. You must be sure that you know the imaging center's and institution's rules and regulations for dealing with an emergency and are willing and able to implement them.

PATIENT TRANSFERRING AND POSITIONING

A patient who is brought to the imaging center will likely be in a wheelchair, on a gurney, or in his or her own bed. While the patient is in your care, be sure that the side rails on the bed or gurney are up or that the patient's seat belt is fastened. This will prevent accidental injuries from falls. If you are performing a CT or

MRI scan, it is your responsibility to help the patient move to the patient couch/gantry.

You must evaluate each patient individually. Determine if he or she feels dizzy or weak. If the patient is as big or bigger than you are, it is best to get help. Be sure to wear a back support belt whenever you move a patient. This will help avoid a painful back injury. Once the patient is on the instrument gantry, you must help position him or her to obtain an optimum image.

CONTRAST AGENTS

The purpose of contrast media is to visualize structures or disease processes that would otherwise be invisible with conventional X ray or CT scans. Barium is used to outline the digestive tract, and iodine in solution is used in most other radioopaque (impenetrable by radiation) media. Ideally the radioopaque medium should be pharmacologically inert; that is, it should not have negative side effects. Unfortunately, this has not been completely achieved. Some patients will experience a feeling of warmth spreading over the body as the medium is injected, and a few will find this objectionable. Concentrated solutions may occasionally cause pain in the upper arm, but this can generally be alleviated by raising the arm at the end of the injection.

Nausea, vomiting, light-headedness, as well as bronchospasm, laryngeal edema, and hypotension, also occur; however, they are relatively rare. You should know what equipment and drugs are available to treat these conditions should they occur. Injection of contrast media outside of a vein can cause pain, so you should be very careful when injecting contrast.

Patients with known allergic reactions are more likely to have an adverse reaction than nonallergic individuals. Infants, elderly patients, and patients with heart disease, as well as those with renal failure, myeloma, and severe diabetes, are also high-risk groups.

DISEASES AND OTHER DISORDERS

HIV

Until 1981 acquired immune deficiency syndrome (AIDS) was virtually an unknown disease. Unfortunately, the number of infected individuals is increasing at an alarming rate. AIDS is most prevalent in homosexual or bisexual males and in intravenous drug abusers, both male and female. But it is being found in increasing numbers of heterosexuals and nonintravenous drug users.

AIDS disrupts the body's immune system. When the immune system is suppressed, the AIDS victim is very susceptible to a variety of deadly *opportunistic* diseases, such as Kaposi's sarcoma, a rare form of skin cancer, or pneumocystis, a parasitic lung disease. A wide variety of drugs have been tested to suppress the AIDS virus and combat the infections and other disorders that typically occur in AIDS patients. No cure has yet been discovered, and researchers do not anticipate a vaccine to prevent infection in the near future. Currently, AIDS is a fatal disease.

AIDS is caused by the human immunodeficiency virus (HIV) and is spread via contact with infected body fluids, such as semen or blood. If you work in an imaging center located in a large inner-city teaching hospital, it is likely that you will encounter patients with HIV on a daily, potentially even an hourly basis. Patients who are bleeding or who might have to be injected with contrast media or a radiopharmaceutical present the most significant risk.

AIDS does not respect ethnic or socioeconomic boundaries. So, even if you do not work in the inner city, it is likely that you will encounter patients with HIV. And you cannot tell, just by looking, whether they are infected or not. They may not even know themselves. So, it is best to assume that they are. If you must deal with someone who is bleeding or you need to give someone an injection, wear gloves and face protection. Also, be careful about sticking yourself with contaminated needles. Dispose of needles and soiled items properly.

Hepatitis B

Hepatitis B, a viral disease that attacks the liver, is spread by contact with blood and other biological fluids. It is not uniformly fatal like AIDS, but people with hepatitis B are more likely to develop liver cancer or cirrhosis of the liver. It is best to take the same precautions with someone suspected of having hepatitis as with AIDS; i.e., wear glove and face protection when giving injections or dealing with situations in which the patient is likely to bleed. There is a vaccine for hepatitis B. Check with a physician to determine whether you should receive it.

Tuberculosis

Until recently, the incidence of tuberculosis has been on the decline since the turn of the century. The decline was apparently caused by improved public health measures and the development of a number of antibiotics. However, the incidence of tuberculosis is now apparently rising. There are currently a number of strains of the tubercle bacilli that are resistant to commonly used antibiotics. And in some cases they are resistant to combinations of antibiotics. These bacilli apparently developed as a result of patients with tuberculosis not completing their antibiotic treatment. If the antibiotic is stopped before all of the bacilli are killed, the ones that remain when the antibiotic treatment is stopped are relatively resistant to the antibiotic and rapidly reproduce. Ultimately, the resistant strains are spread to other individuals.

In contrast to AIDS or hepatitis B, tuberculosis can infect the body via a number of different routes, including the digestive and respiratory tract and the conjunctiva (the "third" eyelid in the corner of your eye). Transmission of tuberculosis is airborne and facilitated by close contact. So, it is important to wash your hands carefully after handling a patient and avoid sneezes and coughs that occur in your direction. If you do catch tuberculosis, be sure to complete your antibiotic treatment, so that you do not add to the resistant strains.

YOU AND THE ELECTROMAGNETIC SPECTRUM

Imaging technology takes advantage of different portions of the electromagnetic spectrum. Physicists picture an electromagnetic wave as being like two sine waves positioned at right angles relative to each other. One of the sine waves represents the electric field; the other, the magnetic field. The sine waves vary in frequency.

The electromagnetic spectrum ranges from extremely low frequencies (ELF) such as the 60-hertz fields and potentials in the overhead power lines that provide the electric energy that powers our electric lights, appliances, and computers, as well as imaging equipment. If electromagnetic waves in the ELF-frequency range have any biological impact (there is considerable controversy about this point right now), most investigators believe that the magnetic field would be responsible.

The electromagnetic spectrum extends to radio-frequency (about 100,000 hertz) and microwave-frequency (about 10 billion hertz) radiation, and to visible light (about 100 trillion hertz). Electromagnetic radiation from ELF through visible light is commonly referred to as *nonionizing radiation;* that is, it does not possess enough energy to cause atoms to ionize.

Ionization means that as radiation passes through matter, such as a human body, and passes close enough to an orbital electron of an atom, it transfers sufficient energy to the electron to remove it from its orbit around the atom. This forms an *ionic pair:* the ionized atom and the released electron. When an atom is ionized, its chemical properties change. If the atom is part of a large molecule, ionization may cause the breakup of the molecule. If the molecule is an enzyme, it may not work anymore. If the molecule is a DNA or RNA molecule, ionization may cause a mutation. Or, the atom may be transformed into a *free radical,* an uncharged molecule containing a single unpaired electron in its outermost shell. Free radicals are very unstable and very reactive. They can pass through the cell membrane and have enough energy to disrupt chemical bonds, as well as produce lesions at some distance from the initially ionized atom.

The effects of electromagnetic radiation in the radio-frequency range (RFR) or microwave-frequency range (MFR) on a living organism are determined by the amount and form of energy that the organism absorbs. In contrast to ELF, if RFR or MFR have some biological impact, it is the electric rather than the magnetic field that is responsible for the effect. At an interface between materials with differing capacities for conducting electricity (such as between air and the surface of the organism), RFR or MFR is either reflected or refracted. The fraction of energy that is not reflected enters the body and undergoes partial or complete absorption. The *attenuation constant* of the material (the rate of energy absorption per unit of distance that the energy travels) is proportional to the square root of the electric conductivity of the material. The attenuation constant and *dielectric constant* (efficiency of a material as an insulator of electric current) vary with the type of material and the frequency of the nonreflected energy.

Living organisms contain many interfaces between different materials (e.g., muscle–fat, body cavity–adjacent tissue), so energy distribution is not homogeneous.

Energy absorption is generally measured in terms of the rate of energy absorption per unit of volume divided by the mass density of the elements in the energy-absorbing object, and is generally expressed in watts per kilogram (W/kg). It is generally agreed that significant effects do not occur until energy absorption reaches 1 W/kg, and hazardous effects do not occur until energy absorption reaches 4 W/kg. These effects are due primarily to increases in body temperature caused by the absorbed energy.

Ultraviolet rays (about one quadrillion hertz) are responsible for the sunburn you receive if you spend too much time in the sunlight. Ultraviolet waves form the upper edge of visible light (some organisms, such as honeybees, can apparently see ultraviolet waves) and possess enough energy (over 10 electron volts) to ionize atoms. Shorter wavelengths, such as X rays or delta rays, possess considerably more energy (over one million electron volts).

SONOGRAM SCANNERS

High-resolution sonographic transducers that are used to resolve small objects, such as parts of the eye, emit frequencies in the 10-megahertz range. Sonographic transducers used to scan larger structures, such as the abdomen, emit frequencies that are in the range of 2.5 megahertz. Their wavelengths are relatively long (from 0.01 to 100 meters) and their energies relatively small (about 0.000001 electron volt). Since diagnostic ultrasound intensities range from 1 to 10 milliwatts per square centimeter, it is very unlikely that they would deposit enough energy to cause a significant change in the temperature of the tissue or organ under investigation. Small increases in local temperature will occur as a result of relaxation processes and molecular friction or agitation, caused by the movement of molecules as the sound wave passes through matter. There have been no reports of manifest (immediately evident) or late effects that have occurred in humans exposed to diagnostic levels of medical ultrasound. The absolute minimum dose to cause significant biological effects in animal models is one hundred milliwatts per square centimeter, at least ten times more powerful than the dose typically used in diagnostic ultrasound, and effects only occurred after many hours of continuous exposure.

RADIONUCLIDE IMAGING

Radioactive isotopes are used in diagnostic imaging because they release gamma rays as they decay (naturally lose their radioactivity). Gamma rays are similar to X rays but occur as a result of decay of the nucleus. To minimize the radiation dose to the patient, imagers use the smallest possible dose of an isotope with a short half-life (the *half-life* of an isotope is the period of time required for a quantity of radioactivity to be reduced to one half of its original value.) The radionuclide technetium-99m is commonly used for thyroid and vascular imaging. It has a half-life of six hours and emits gamma radiation at a suitable energy that allows for easy detection. Technetium-99m can be attached to other molecules that concentrate selectively in different parts of the body. For example, if technetium-99m is tagged with a complex organic phosphate, it will be taken up and concentrated by the bones, thus allowing the skeleton to be visualized. Other radionuclides that are commonly used are indium-111, gallium-67, iodine-123, and thallium-201.

The gamma rays that are emitted by the isotope as it decays are detected by a gamma camera, which consists of a sodium iodide crystal that is attached to a number of photomultiplier tubes. When a gamma ray strikes the sodium iodide crystal, it causes the crystal to emit a photon of light. The light is electrically amplified and converted to an electrical pulse by the photomultiplier tube. The output of the tube is attached to a computer that allows further manipulation and enhancement of the signal. If the gamma camera moves around the patient, the process is called single photon emission computed tomography, the SPECT technique mentioned earlier.

CT SCAN

The CT scan allows very small differences in X-ray absorption to be visualized. The range of densities of a typical X-ray film produced by conventional radiology is about 20, but the range of densities in a CT scan of the same structures is about 2,000. The computer can calculate the absorption value of each picture element, or pixel. Each pixel is 0.25 to 0.6 millimeters in diameter (depending on the resolution of the scanner) and varies in thickness from 1 to 10 millimeters.

Images produced through CT scans are often distorted by the presence of radiating linear streaks. These streaks make it harder to look at surrounding structures. They are generally caused by movement of the patient (remember, the exposure is typically one to two seconds long) or by objects with very high density.

Ionizing radiation from X rays or gamma rays is potentially harmful, especially to dividing cells. Unnecessary exposure to X rays or gamma rays should be avoided, especially since their effects tend to be cumulative.

The World Health Organization—Basic Radiological System Advisory Group recommends that you should always do the following:

1. Stand behind the control panel when an X-ray exposure is made.
2. Wear lead aprons and lead gloves if a patient needs to be held.

3. Do not allow anyone to remain in the room except the patient.
4. Always wear your film badge or other dosimeter (radiation-measuring device), and have it checked regularly.
5. Never perform any scan unless ordered by a physician.

Remember, X rays can harm you even though you cannot see them or feel them. But also remember that X rays are only dangerous if you are careless.

Film badges were introduced in the mid-1940s. They consist of a small piece of radiographic film sandwiched between two metal (usually aluminum or copper) filters inside a plastic holder. Film badges should be worn with their proper side to the front. Film badges should not be worn for more than one month, since heat and humidity will alter their sensitivity. Film badges are sensitive to exposures of less than twenty megaroentgens.

Thermoluminescent dosimeters contain lithium fluoride in crystal form. These dosimeters cost about twice as much as film dosimeters. But they are more sensitive (over five megaroentgens) and can be worn for as long as three months. If the lithium fluoride is exposed to radiation, the crystal absorbs the energy and stores it in the form of excited electrons in the crystal. If the crystal is heated, the excited electrons fall back to their normal state, which causes the emission of visible light. The intensity of the light, as measured by a photomultiplier tube, is proportional to the radiation dose to which the crystal was exposed.

Pocket ionization chambers are generally two centimeters in diameter and ten centimeters long and are clipped to clothing like a writing pen. This dosimeter must be charged to a predetermined voltage. When the dosimeter is exposed to radiation, the charge is dissipated and neutralized. The typical range of the dosimeter is up to two hundred milliroentgens. If exposure exceeds this range, the precise level of exposure might be difficult to determine.

MRI SCANS

MRI scans can be directly reconstructed in any plane. MRI scans are relatively slow when compared to CT scans (several minutes as opposed to a few seconds). The patient must remain still for this time. Unavoidable movements such as breathing tend to degrade the image. MRI does not require a source of ionizing radiation. But all MRI imagers have strong static magnetic fields. The Bureau of Radiologic Health (BRH), the federal agency responsible for establishing safety standards, recommends an upper limit of two tesla, because harmful biological or genetic effects have not been observed below this level. Static magnetic fields well above this level (such as twenty-four tesla) can cause changes in the electric activity of nerves and the heart.

On the other hand, ferromagnetic objects (objects that make a good magnet) can be potentially dangerous to you and your patient when the static field is turned on. No metallic object should be allowed in the MRI room unless it is carefully checked to determine its response to strong magnetic fields. Electronic metal detectors, much like those used at airports, can be used to detect metal objects on or in the patient or any accompanying persons. Unfortunately, metal detectors are not sensitive to small objects, so there is no substitute for a careful and detailed history of the patient and a careful inspection of the patient with a small magnet to detect small metal objects. Fortunately, most surgically implanted stainless steel devices (like aneurysm clips and prostheses) are relatively nonmagnetic, but there is a wide range.

Cardiac pacemakers may be adversely affected. The switch that permits external control of common pacemakers is magnetically controlled. Also, ferromagnetic components of the pacemaker may be attracted by the field and cause the pacemaker to reposition itself.

MRI scanners also produce alternating magnetic fields, which can induce electric currents in the patient's tissues and in metallic objects within or adjacent to the patient. The BRH recommends the upper limits for such magnetic fields to be three tesla per second.

MRI scanners also produce radio-frequency radiation that ranges in frequency from one to one hundred megahertz. RFR can cause heating of the tissue, due to induced electric currents, as well as atomic and molecular oscillations. The quantity of current produced is proportional to the square of the RFR frequency and is also proportional to the square of the diameter of the subject. Superficial tissues will typically receive the greatest amount of heat. Human studies have reported that the temperature increase is about one degree Celsius, which is within the normal daily variation in temperature. When the alternating magnetic field is turned on, a relatively loud sound (sixty-five to ninety-five decibels) is produced.

Medium-high and high MRI scanners use superconducting magnets. These superconducting magnets require cryogens (liquid helium or nitrogen) to cool them to allow them to develop superconductivity. These liquid and gaseous elements are dangerous. They are very cold and can cause frostbite. Cryogen spills or quenching of the magnet can release large amounts of cryogen gases that can replace oxygen and asphyxiate those in the immediate vicinity.

It is not currently clear what impact, if any, the static and alternating magnetic fields might have on a pregnant female or her fetus. The Food and Drug Administration has not given approval for the routine MRI scans of pregnant females.

EARLY EFFECTS OF IONIZING RADIATION
(RADIATION SICKNESS)

Most experts agree that exposure should not exceed 5,000 milliroentgens annually. The lethal dose that kills 50 percent of the individuals exposed to it within thirty days (commonly called the $LD_{50/30}$ dose) is a single exposure of about 300 rads if no post-exposure supportive treatment is provided, and about 850 rads if postexposure treatment is provided. If you know and follow standard safety standards, your exposure should never come close to this amount.

Acute radiation-induced human lethality is very unlikely to occur in an imaging setting because the X rays and gamma rays are neither sufficiently intense nor large enough to cause death. Some accidental exposures in the nuclear weapon or nuclear energy fields have occurred. The acute radiation syndrome occurs following high-level whole-body exposure to radiation and consists of three syndromes: *hematologic, gastrointestinal,* and *neuromuscular.* Which of these three syndromes occurs depends on the dose of radiation.

With all three syndromes there is a prodromal phase that consists of clinical symptoms that occur within hours of high-level radiation exposure and continue for one or two days. This is followed by a latent period that can last hours (in cases of exposure to over 5,000 rads) to weeks (with 100 to 500 rads). During the latent phase, there is no clinical sign of radiation sickness. The latent phase is followed by a period of manifest radiation sickness.

The prodromal phases of the hematologic syndrome (which follows exposure to 200 to 1,000 rads) include nausea, vomiting, diarrhea, and a decrease of white blood cells in the blood. Following the latent phase, the manifest illness of the hematologic syndrome is characterized by a continued reduction in the numbers of white and red cells, as well as platelets. If the radiation dose was sufficiently high, the reduction in blood cells will continue unchecked until the body's defenses against infections and other disorders is nil. If the radiation dose is not lethal, recovery can begin within two to four weeks of exposure and last as long as six months.

If the radiation dose is 1,000 to 5,000 rads, the gastrointestinal syndrome will follow the latent period. This is characterized by a second wave of vomiting and diarrhea, as well as a loss of appetite and lethargy. The diarrhea will increase in severity and will lead to loose, then watery and bloody stools. Death usually occurs as a result of severe damage to the cells lining the intestines.

If the dose is in excess of 5,000 rads, the central nervous system syndrome occurs. This prodromal phase is characterized by severe vomiting and nausea. The person will also be extremely nervous and confused and will complain of loss of vision and a burning sensation in the skin. This is followed by a latent period of six to twelve hours, during which the symptoms will decrease in intensity or disappear. After the latent period, the symptoms of the prodromal phase will reappear with greater intensity. They will be accompanied by disorientation and loss of muscle coordination. The person may have difficulty breathing and may have one or more convulsions. Ultimately, he or she will become lethargic, lapse into a coma, and die. The principal causes of death are an elevated fluid content in the brain, changes in the blood vessels in the brain, and inflammation of the meninges.

BIBLIOGRAPHY

EXAM REVIEWS AND PREPARATION

Bushong, S. C. *Magnetic Resonance Imaging: Study Guide and Exam Review.* Mosby-Year Book, 1995.

Craig, M. *Ultrasound Exam Review: Sonographer's Self Assessment Guide.* Lippincott, Williams, and Wilkins, 1994.

Edelman, S. K. *Understanding Ultrasound Physics: Fundamentals and Exam Review.* Educational Sonographic Professional, Inc., 1994.

Meacham, K. S. *The MRI Study Guide for Technologists.* Springer Verlag, 1995.

Odwin, C. S., T. Dubinsky, and A. C. Fleischer. *Appleton & Lange's Review for the Ultrasonography Examination.* Appleton and Lange, 1993.

Pierce, M. F. and R. Carnovale. *Comprehensive Review for the Radiology Registry: A Centralized Resource.* Lippincott, Williams, and Wilkins, 1998.

Rumwell, C. and M. M. McPharlin. *Vascular Technology: An Illustrated Guide for the Registry.* Davies, Inc., 1996.

Saia, D. *Appleton & Lange's Review for the Radiography Examination.* Appleton and Lange, 1996.

———. *Radiography: Program Review and Exam Preparation.* Appleton and Lange, 1996.

Widmer, R. S. and K. W. van Soelen. *Radiography Study Guide and Registry Review.* W. B. Saunders, 1999.

TECHNOLOGISTS

Bushong, S. C. *Radiologic Science for Technologists: Physics, Biology, and Protection.* Mosby-Year Book, 1997.

Durand, K. S. *Critical Thinking: Developing Skills in Radiography.* F. A. Davis, 1999.

MacE, J. D. and N. Kowalzzk. *Radiographic Pathology for Technologists.* Mosby-Year Book, 1997.

Parelli, R. J. *Radiologic Technology Clinical Manual.* Saint Lucie Press, 1997.

Selman, J. *The Fundamental of Physics and Radiobiology for the Radiologic Technologist.* Charles C. Thomas, 2000.

Woodward, P. and R. D. Freimarck. *MRI Guide for Technologists.* McGraw Hill, 1994.

COMPUTED TOMOGRAPHY

Cahill, D. R. and M. J. Orland. *Atlas of Human Cross Sectional Anatomy: With CT and MR Images.* John Wiley and Sons, 1995.

Lee, J. K. T., S. S. Sagel, and R. J. Stanley. *Computed Body Tomography with MRI Correlation.* Lippincott, Williams, and Wilkins, 1998.

Slone, R. M., A. J. Fisher, and A. A. Fisher. *Pocket Guide to Body CT Differential Diagnosis.* McGraw Hill, 1999.

MRI

Brown, M. A. and R. C. Smelka. *MRI: Basic Principles and Applications.* Wiley-Liss, 1999.

Bushong, S. C. *Magnetic Resonance Imaging: Physical and Biological Principles.* Mosby-Year Book, 1995.

Rajan, S. S. *MRI: A Conceptual Overview.* Springer Verlag, 1997.

Reimer, P. R., P. M. Parizel, and F. A. Stichnoth. *Clinical MR-Imaging: A Practical Approach.* Springer Verlag, 1999.

SONOGRAPHY

Duck, F. A., A. C. Baker, and H. C. Starritt. *Ultrasound in Medicine.*
Institute of Physics Publication, 1998.
Feigenbaum, H. *Echocardiography.* Lea & Febiger, 1995.
Kremkau, F. W. and A. Allen. *Diagnostic Ultrasound: Principles and
Instruments.* W. B. Saunders, 1998.
McGahan, J. P. and B. B. Goldberg. *Diagnostic Ultrasound: A Logical
Approach.* Lippincott, Williams, and Wilkins, 1998.

INTERVENTIONAL AND FUNCTIONAL IMAGING

Jolesz, F. A. and I. R. Young. *Interventional MRI: Techniques and
Clinical Experience.* Mosby, 1998.
Krishnan, K. R. R. and P. M. Doraiswamy. *Brain Imaging in Clinical
Psychiatry.* Marcel Dekker, Inc., 1997.
Lufkin, R. B. *Interventional MRI.* Mosby, 1999.
Moonen, C. T. W. and P. A. Bandettini. *Functional MRI.* Springer Verlag,
1999.
Von Schulthess, G. K. and J. Hennig. *Functional Imaging.* Lippincott-
Raven, 1998.

NUCLEAR MEDICINE

Bernier, D. R., P. E. Christian, and J. K. Langan. *Nuclear Medicine:
Technology and Techniques.* Mosby, 1997.
Peters, A. M. and M. J. Myers. *Physiological Measurements with
Radionuclides in Clinical Practice.* Oxford University Press, 1998.

SAFETY

Statkiewicz-Sherer, M. A., P. J. Visconti, and E. R. Ritenour. *Radiation
Protection in Medical Radiography.* Mosby, 1998.

SELECTED IMAGING PERIODICALS

American Journal of Neuroradiology, bimonthly
American Journal of Roentgenology, monthly
Computerized Medical Imaging and Graphics, bimonthly
Current Problems in Diagnostic Radiology, bimonthly
*Echocardiography: A Journal of Cardiovascular
Ultrasound and Allied Techniques,* bimonthly
Investigative Radiology, monthly
Journal of Computer-Assisted Tomography, bimonthly
Journal of Diagnostic Medical Sonography, biennial
Journal of Magnetic Resonance, monthly
Journal of Neuroimaging, quarterly
Journal of Nuclear Medicine, monthly
Journal of Nuclear Medicine Technology, quarterly
Journal of Ultrasound in Medicine, monthly
Journal of Vascular and Interventional Radiology, quarterly
Magnetic Resonance Imaging, bimonthly
Nuclear Medicine and Biology, published eight times a year
Physics in Medicine and Biology, monthly
RadioGraphics, bimonthly
Radiologic Technology, bimonthly
Radiological Clinics of North America, monthly
Radiology, monthly
Radiology Management, quarterly
Roentgenological Briefs, quarterly
Seminars in Nuclear Medicine, quarterly
Ultrasound in Medicine and Biology, published
nine times a year

ORGANIZATION AND AGENCY ACRONYMS

ABNM	American Board of Nuclear Medicine
ABR	American Board of Radiology
AMA	American Medical Association
ARDMS	American Registry of Diagnostic Medical Sonographers
ARRT	American Registry of Radiologic Technologists
CAHEA	Committee of Allied Health Education and Accreditation
NMTCB	Nuclear Medicine and Technology Certification Board

PROFESSIONAL ORGANIZATIONS AND ADDRESSES

ACCREDITATION

Commission on Accreditation of Allied Health Education Programs
  (CAAHEP)
American Medical Association
515 N. State St.
Chicago, IL 60610
http://www.caahep.org

The Commission on Accreditation of Allied Health Education Programs (CAAHEP) was established as a nonprofit agency on July 1, 1994. It remains the largest specialized accreditation system in the country, accrediting allied health educational programs in eighteen disciplines. The CAAHEP accredits nearly two thousand allied health education programs sponsored by more than one thousand institutions across the nation, including universities and colleges, academic health centers, junior and community colleges, hospitals, clinics, blood banks, vocational-technical schools, proprietary institutions, and U.S. government institutions and agencies.

REGISTRATION/CERTIFICATION

American Registry of Diagnostic Medical Sonographers (ARDMS)
    2368 Victory Pkwy., # 510
    Cincinnati, OH 45206-2810
    Founded 1975
    Members: 11,000

The ARDMS is the national certifying agency for and registry of certified technologists in the field of diagnostic medical sonography and vascular technology. The ARDMS publishes the *American Registry of Diagnostic Medical Sonographers Directory* (annual) and an *Informational Brochure* (annual).

American Registry of Radiologic Technologists (ARRT)
    1255 Northland Dr.
    Mendota Heights, MN 55120
    Founded 1922

The ARRT is the national certifying agency for and registry of certified radiographers, as well as nuclear medicine technologists and radiation therapy technologists, who are listed in the *ARRT Directory*. The ARRT also offers advanced-level examinations in mammography and cardiovascular-interventional technology.

Nuclear Medicine Technology Certification Board (NMTCB)
    2970 Clairmont Rd., Suite 935
    Atlanta, GA 30329
    Founded 1977
    Members: 12,000
    http://www.nmtcb.org

The NMTCB is the national certifying agency for and registry of certified nuclear medical technologists. The NMTCB publishes the *Certification Examination Validation Report* (annual) and the *NMTCB Directory* (annual).

PROFESSIONAL ORGANIZATIONS—IMAGING

Computerized Medical Imaging Society (CMIS)
c/o National Biomedical Research Foundation
Georgetown University Medical Center
3900 Reservoir Rd. NW
Washington, DC 20007
Founded 1976
Members: 400

The CMIS provides a forum for physicians and other medical personnel to exchange information concerning the medical use of computerized tomography in radiologic diagnosis. The CMIS publishes *Computerized Medical Imaging and Graphics* (bimonthly).

Council on Diagnostic Imaging (CODI)
P.O. Box 1655
Ashtabula, OH 44004
Founded 1936
Members: 4,500

CODI is the professional society of chiropractic roentgenologists, educators, students, and chiropractors interested in roentgenology. CODI publishes *Roentgenological Briefs* (quarterly).

Society of Computed Body Tomography and Magnetic Resonance
(SCBTMR)
c/o Matrix Meetings
P.O. Box 1026
Rochester, MN 55903-1026
Founded 1977
Members: 97

The SCBTMR provides information on computed tomography and magnetic resonance imaging through lectures, workshops, seminars, and case presentations.

Society of Diagnostic Medical Sonographers (SODMS)
    12770 Coit Rd., Suite 508
    Dallas, TX 75251
    Founded 1970
    Members: 12,000

The SODMS seeks to advance the science of diagnostic medical sonography, establish and maintain high standards of education, and provide an identity and sense of direction for their membership, which includes sonographers, physician sonologists, and others who utilize high-frequency sound for diagnostic purposes. The SODMS publishes the *Journal of Diagnostic Medical Sonography* (biennial).

Society for Magnetic Resonance Imaging (SMRI)
    213 W. Institute Pl., Suite 501
    Chicago, IL 60610
    Founded 1982
    Members: 1,700

The SMRI promotes the applications of magnetic resonance techniques to medicine and biology, with special emphasis on imaging. The SMRI publishes the *Journal of Magnetic Resonance Imaging* (bimonthly) and *Echoes* (three times a year).

OTHER PROFESSIONAL ORGANIZATIONS

American Association of Medical Dosimetrists (AAMD)
    c/o Credentialling Services, Inc.
    P.O. Box 1498
    Galesburg, IL 61401
    Founded: 1976
    Members: 1,000

AAMD publishes the *Medical Physics Journal.*

American Association for Women Radiologists (AAWR)
  1891 Preston White Dr.
  Reston, VA 22901
  Founded: 1981
  Members: 1,770

AAWR publishes a newsletter and a membership directory.

American Board of Nuclear Medicine (ABNM)
  900 Veteran Ave.
  Los Angeles, CA 90024-1786
  Founded 1971
  Members: 12

The ABNM is sponsored by the American Board of Internal Medicine, the American Board of Pathology, and the American Board of Radiology and the Society of Nuclear Medicine and establishes requirements for specialty board certification for physicians in nuclear medicine. The ABNM conducts examinations, issues certificates, and maintains a registry of certificate holders, as well as aids in the assessment and accreditation of nuclear medicine programs in hospitals and institutions offering graduate training. The ABNM publishes the *American Board of Nuclear Medicine Information, Policies and Procedures* (annual).

American Board of Radiology (ABR)
  5255 E. Williams Circle, Suite 3200
  Tucson, AR 85711
  Founded 1934
  Members: 23

The ABR certifies physicians in the specialty of diagnostic radiology and radiation oncology, and physicists in radiologic physics and related branches, by establishing qualifications and conducting examinations.

American College of Nuclear Medicine (ACNM)
    P.O. Box 175
    Landisville, PA 17538
    Founded 1972
    Members: 369

The ACNM encourages improved and continuing education for practitioners in nuclear medicine, thereby improving its benefits to patients. The ACNM also fosters the study of socioeconomic aspects of the practice of nuclear medicine. The organization bestows Gold Medal Awards and publishes the *ACNM Directory* (biennial) and *ACNM Report* (bimonthly).

American College of Nuclear Physicians (ACNP)
    1101 Connecticut Ave. NW, Suite 700
    Washington, DC 20036
    Founded 1974
    Members: 1,700

The ACNP seeks to foster the highest standards of nuclear medicine service and consultations to the public, hospitals, and referring physicians, to promote the continuing competence of practitioners of nuclear medicine, and to improve the socioeconomic aspects of the practice of nuclear medicine. The ACNP publishes the *Directory* (annual) and *Scanner* (ten times a year).

American College of Podiatric Radiologists (ACPR)
    169 Lincoln Rd., # 308
    Miami Beach, FL 33139
    Founded 1944
    Members: 80

The ACPR is a professional society of podiatrists interested in the use and interpretation of X rays in treating ailments of the lower extremities. The ACPR publishes a *Newsletter* (two to four times a year) and *Post Convention Reports* (one to two times a year).

American College of Radiology (ACR)
   1891 Preston White Dr.
   Reston, VA 22091
   Founded 1923
   Members: 30,000

The ACR is a professional society of physicians and radiologic physicists who specialize in the use of X ray, ultrasound, nuclear medicine magnetic resonance, and other imaging techniques for the diagnosis of disease and the treatment and management of cancer. The ACR publishes books, booklets, pamphlets, textbooks, reprints, kits, films, and slides, and the *Bulletin* (monthly) and the *ACR Directory* (annual).

American Healthcare Radiology Administrators (AHRA)
   P.O. Box 334
   Sudbury, MA 01776
   Founded 1973
   Members: 3,775

The AHRA seeks to improve management of radiology departments in hospitals and other health care facilities and to provide a forum for publication of educational, scientific, and professional materials. The AHRA publishes *Radiology Management* (quarterly) and the bibliography for the *Radiology Administrator.*

American Institute of Ultrasound in Medicine (AIUM)
   14750 Sweitzer Ln., Suite 100
   Laurel, MD 20707
   Founded 1955
   Members: 11,000

The AIUM seeks to promote the application of ultrasound in clinical medicine, diagnosis, and research; the study of the effect of ultrasound on tissue; and the development of standards for its applications. AIUM publishes the *Journal of Ultrasound in Medicine* and the *AIUM Reporter.*

American Medical Association, Section Council on Radiology (AMA)
    1891 Preston White Dr.
    Reston, VA 20901

American Osteopathic College of Radiology (AOCR)
    119 E. Second St.
    Milan, MO 63556
    Founded 1940
    Members: 840

The AOCR is an organization composed of certified radiologists, residents-in-training, and others active in the field of radiology. The AOCR publishes the *AOCR Membership Directory* (annual) and *Viewbox* (quarterly).

American Radiological Nurses Association (ARNA)
    2021 Spring Rd., Suite 600
    Oak Brook, IL 60523
    Founded: 1981
    Members: 1,543

American Roentgen Ray Society (ARRS)
    44211 Slatestone Ct.
    Leesburg, VA 20176

The ARRS is an organization of specialists in diagnostic and therapeutic roentgenology and publishes the *American Journal of Roentgenology* (monthly) and the *ARRS Membership Directory* (annual).

American Society of Clinic Radiologists (ASCR)
    Kelsey-Seybold Clinic, P.A.
    6624 Fannin St., Suite 1800
    Houston, TX 77030
    Founded 1977
    Members: 21 clinics

The ASCR seeks to maintain and improve the quality and efficiency of radiologic care, as well as to help radiologists share information about educational, operational, technical, political, and socioeconomic aspects of radiologic practice.

American Society of Neuroradiology (ASNR)
  2210 Midwest Rd., Suite 207
  Oak Brook, IL 60521
  Founded 1962
  Members: 2,028

The ASNR seeks to foster education, basic science research, and communication in neuroradiology and publishes the *American Journal of Neuroradiology* (bimonthly) and the *ASNR Membership Roll* (annual).

American Society for Therapeutic Radiology and Oncology (ASTRO)
  1891 Preston White Dr.
  Reston, VA 20191
  Founded 1955
  Members: 4,500

ASTRO seeks to extend the benefits of radiation therapy to patients with cancer or other disorders, as well as to advance the scientific basis of radiation therapy. ASTRO publishes *The International Journal of Radiation Oncology, Biology, and Physics* (periodic), the *ASTRO Membership Directory* (annual), and the *ASTRO Newsletter* (periodic).

Association of Educators in Radiological Sciences, Inc. (AERS)
  2021 Spring Rd., Suite 600
  Oak Brook, IL 60521
  Founded: 1967
  Members: 645

AERS publishes *Radiologic Science and Education.*

Association of University Radiologists (AUR)
  2021 Spring Rd., Suite 600
  Oak Brook, IL 60523
  Founded 1953
  Members: 1,209

The AUR seeks to provide a forum for university-based radiologists to present and discuss results of research, teaching, and administrative issues, as well as to encourage excellence in laboratory and clinical investigation and teaching. The AUR publishes *Investigative Radiology* (monthly).

Conference of Radiation Control Program Directors (CRCPD)
205 Capital Ave.
Frankfort, KY 40601-2832
Founded 1968
Members: 437

The CRCPD seeks to promote radiologic health and uniform radiation control laws and regulations, supports radiation control programs, provides assistance with members' technical work and development, and encourages cooperation between enforcement programs and agencies at state and federal levels. The CRCPD publishes the *Directory of Personnel Responsible for Radiological Health Programs* (annual), the *National Conference on Radiation Control—Proceedings* (annual), the *Profile of State and Local Radiation Control Programs in the U.S.* (annual), and the *CRCPD Newsletter* (quarterly).

International Association of Dento-Maxillo-Facial Radiology (IADMFR)
UTHSC Dental School
Dental Diagnostic Sciences
7703 Floyd Curl Dr.
San Antonio, TX 78284
Founded 1968
Members: 500

The IADMFR seeks to promote the advancement of radiologic research, teaching, and clinical service relating to dental and facial care. The IADMFR publishes the *Journal of Dento-Maxillo-Facial Radiology* (four times a year), the *Newsletter* (semiannual), and the *Proceedings* (triennial).

International Commission on Radiation Units and Measurements (ICRU)
7910 Woodmont Ave., Suite 800
Bethesda, MD 20814
Founded 1925
Members: 101

The ICRU develops internationally acceptable recommendations dealing with quantities and units of radiation and radionuclides, as well as procedures suitable for the measurement and application of these quantities in clinical radiology and radiobiology. The ICRU publishes *ICRU Reports* (periodic).

International Organization for Medical Physics (IOMP)
Gershenson Radiation Oncology Center
Harper Hospital
3990 John R. St.
Detroit, MI 48201
Founded: 1963
Members: 12,000

IOMP publishes *Physics in Medicine and Biology, Clinical Physics and Physiological Measurement,* and *Medical Physics World.*

International Skeletal Society (ISS)
University of California, San Francisco
Department of Radiology
San Francisco, CA 94143
Founded 1973
Members: 330

The ISS seeks to advance the science of skeletal radiology by bringing together radiologists and individuals in related disciplines and by providing continuing education courses. The ISS publishes *Skeletal Radiology* (eight times a year), a *Membership Directory* (annual), and a *Newsletter* (three times a year).

International Society for Magnetic Resonance in Medicine, Inc.
(ISMRM)
2118 Milvia St., Suite 201
Berkeley, CA 94704
Founded: 1994
Members: 5,100

ISMRM was formed in 1993 as a merger between the Society of Magnetic Resonance in Medicine and the Society for Magnetic Resonance Imaging. It publishes *MR Pulse, Magnetic Resonance in Medicine,* and the *Journal of Magnetic Resonance Imaging.*

International Society of Radiographers and Radiological Technologists
    (ISRRT)
    52 Addison Crescent
    Don Mills, Ontario
    M3B 1K8
    Canada
    Founded: 1959
    Members: 11,000

National Council on Radiation Protection and Measurements (NCRPM)
    7910 Woodmont Ave., Suite 800
    Bethesda, MD 20814
    Founded: 1929
    Members: 75

National Medical Association, Inc., Section on Radiology (NMA)
    c/o Samuel W. McFadden, M.D.
    Tobey Hospital, Department of Radiology
    43 High St.
    Wareham, MA 02571
    Founded: 1949
    Members: 320

Radiation Outreach Foundation (ROF)
    3415 Sacramento St.
    San Francisco, CA 94118
    Founded: 1988
    Members: na

Radiological Society of North America (RSNA)
    2021 Spring Rd., Suite 600
    Oak Brook, IL 60521
    Founded 1915
    Members: 30,000

The RSNA promotes the study and practical application of radiology, radium, electricity, and other branches of physics related to medical science, and publishes the *Directory of Members* (annual), *Radiographics* (bimonthly), and *RSNA Today* (bimonthly).

Radiology Research and Education Foundation (RREF)
    3415 Sacramento St.
    San Francisco, CA 94118
    Founded: 1974
    Members: na

Society of Cardiovascular and Interventional Radiology (SCVIR)
    10201 Lee Hwy., Suite 160
    Fairfax, VA 22030
    Founded 1973
    Members: 3,000

The SCVIR seeks to facilitate the exchange of new ideas and techniques and provide educational courses for all physicians working in the field of cardiovascular and interventional radiology. The SCVIR publishes the *Journal of Vascular and Interventional Radiology* (quarterly), the *SCVIR Membership Directory* (annual), the *SCVIR Newsletter* (bimonthly), and the *Directory of Angiography and Interventional Radiology Fellowship Programs and SCVIR News.*

Society of Nuclear Medicine (SNM)
    1850 Samuel Morse Dr.
    Reston, VA 20190
    Founded 1954
    Members: 13,000

The SNM disseminates information concerning nuclear medicine, nuclear magnetic resonance, and the use of radioactive isotopes in the diagnosis and treatment of disease. The SNM oversees the Technologist Section of the Society of Nuclear Medicine, as well as publishing the *Journal of Nuclear Medicine* (monthly) and the *Society of Nuclear Medicine Membership Directory* (every three years).

Society of Nuclear Medicine—Technologist Section (TSSNM)
    136 Madison Ave.
    New York, NY 10016
    Founded 1970
    Members: 4,800

The TSSNM seeks to promote the continued development and improvement of nuclear medicine technology and develop a forum for the exchange of ideas and information. The TSSNM represents the field in areas of licensure, accreditation, and certification. The TSSNM publishes the *Journal of Nuclear Medicine Technology* (quarterly) and the *Membership Directory* (biennial).

Society of Radiologists in Ultrasound (SRU)
    44211 Slatestone Ct.
    Leesburg, VA 20176
    Founded: 1975
    Members: 827

CANADIAN ORGANIZATIONS

Canadian Association of Medical Radiation Technologists (CAMRT)
    294 Albert St., Suite 601
    Ottawa, Ontario
    K1P 6E6
    Canada
    Founded: 1942
    Members: 10,000

CAMRT publishes the *Canadian Journal of Medical Radiation Technology* and the *CAMRT News.*

Canadian Association of Physicists, Medical and Biological Physics
    (CAP)
    150 Lewis Pasteur, Suite 112
    Ottawa, Ontario
    K1N 6N5
    Canada
    Founded: 1954
    Members: 50

    CAP publishes *Physics in Canada.*

Canadian Association of Radiologists (CAR)
    5101 Buchan St., Suite 510
    Montreal, Quebec
    H4P 2R9
    Canada
    Founded: 1937
    Members: 1,700

    CAR publishes the *Forum* (newsletter) and the *Canadian Association of Radiologists' Journal.*

Canadian College of Physicists in Medicine (CCPM)
    c/o Canadian Centre for the Southern Interior
    399 Royal Ave.
    Kelowna, British Columbia
    V1Y 5L3
    Canada
    Founded: 1979
    Members: 136

    CCPM publishes the *Canadian Medical Physics Newsletter.*

Canadian Society of Diagnostic Medical Sonographers (CSDMS)
    P.O. Box 1624
    Yellowknife, Northwest Territories
    X1A 2P2
    Canada

ACCREDITED NUCLEAR MEDICINE TECHNOLOGIST PROGRAMS

UNITED STATES

Alabama

University of Alabama
  at Birmingham
School of Health Related
  Professions
Nuclear Medicine Tech.
  Program
UAB Station,
  SHRP 333 A1
1714 Ninth Avenue S.
Birmingham, AL 35294

Arizona

Gateway Community College
Nuclear Medicine Tech.
  Program
108 N. Fortieth St.
Phoenix, AZ 85034

Arkansas

Baptist Medical System
Nuclear Medicine Tech.
  Program
11900 Colonel Glenn Rd.
Suite 1000
Little Rock, AR 72210

University of Arkansas
  for Medical Sciences
Nuclear Medicine Tech.
  Program
4301 W. Markam, Slot 714
Little Rock, AR 72205

California

California State University—
  Dominguez Hills
Nuclear Medicine Tech.
  Program
1000 E. Victoria St.
Carson, CA 90747

Charles R. Drew University
of Medicine and Science
Nuclear Medicine Tech.
Program
1621 E. 120th St.
Keck Bldg., Room 205
Los Angeles, CA 90059

Loma Linda University
Nuclear Medicine Tech.
Program
Nichol Hall,
Room A-829
Loma Linda, CA 92350

Connecticut

Gateway Community Technical
College
Nuclear Medicine Tech.
Program
88 Bassett Rd.
North Haven, CT 06473

Delaware

Delaware Technical
and Community
College
Nuclear Medicine Tech.
Program
333 Shipley St.
Wilmington, DE 19801

Florida

Broward Community
College
Bldg. 41, Room 137
1000 Coconut Creek Blvd.
Coconut Creek, FL 33066

Halifax Medical Center
Nuclear Medicine Tech.
Program
303 N. Clyde Morris Blvd.
P.O. Box 2830
Daytona Beach, FL 32120-2830

Hillsborough Community College
Nuclear Medicine Tech.
Program
P.O. Box 30030
Tampa, FL 33630

Mt. Sinai Medical Center
of Greater Miami
Nuclear Medicine Tech.
Program
4300 Alton Rd.
Miami Beach, FL 33140

Santa Fe Community College
Nuclear Medicine Tech.
Program
3000 NW Eighty-third St.
Gainesville, FL 32602

University of Miami—Jackson
Memorial Medical Center
Nuclear Medicine Tech.
Program
1611 NW Twelfth Ave.,
Room 237
Miami, FL 33136

Georgia

Medical College of Georgia
Nuclear Medicine Tech.
Program
School of Allied Health
Sciences AE 1003
Augusta, GA 30912

Illinois

College of Du Page
  Nuclear Medicine Tech.
  Program
  425 Twenty-second St.
  Glen Ellyn, IL 60137-6599

Edward Hines Jr., Veterans
  Administration Hospital
  Nuclear Medicine Tech.
  Program—115F
  Fifth Avenue
  & Roosevelt Rd.
  Hines, IL 60141

Triton College
  Nuclear Medicine Tech.
  Program
  2000 Fifth Ave.
  River Grove, IL 60171

Indiana

Ball State University
  Methodist Hospital
  Allied Health
  Department
  Nuclear Medicine
  Technology
  P.O. Box 1367
  Indianapolis, IN 46202

Indiana University School
  of Medicine
  Nuclear Medicine Tech.
  Program
  541 Clinical Dr. CL 120
  Indianapolis, IN 46202

Iowa

University of Iowa
  Hospitals and Clinics
  Department of Radiology,
  3800 JPP
  Division of Nuclear Medicine
  200 Hawkins Dr.
  Iowa City, IA 52240

Kansas

University of Kansas
  Medical Center
  Program of Nuclear Medicine
  3901 Rainbow Blvd.
  Kansas City, KS 66160-7234

Kentucky

Lexington Community College
  Nuclear Medicine Technology
  330-A Oswald Building,
  Cooper Dr.
  Lexington, KY 40506-0235

University of Louisville
  Nuclear Medicine Tech.
  Program
  K Bldg. #4056, HSC
  Louisville, KY 40292

Louisiana

Delgado Community College
  Nuclear Medicine Tech.
  Program
  615 City Park Ave.
  New Orleans, LA 70119

Overton Brooks Veterans
    Administration Medical
    Center
Nuclear Medicine Tech.
    Program
510 E. Stoner Ave.
Shreveport, LA 71101-4295

Maryland

Essex Community College
Nuclear Medicine Tech.
    Program
7201 Rossville Blvd.
Baltimore, MD 21237

The Johns Hopkins Hospital
Nuclear Medicine Tech.
    Program
Radiology
    Administration Blalock
    B-179
600 N. Wolfe St.
Baltimore, MD 21287

Naval School of Health
    Sciences—MD
Nuclear Medicine Tech.
    School
8901 Wisconsin Ave.
Bethesda, MD 20889-5033

Prince George's Community
    College
Nuclear Medicine Tech.
    Program
301 Largo Rd.
Largo, MD 20772

Massachusetts

Bunker Hill Community
    College
Nuclear Medicine Tech.
    Program
New Rutherford Ave.
Boston, MA 02129

Massachusetts College
    of Pharmacy
    and Allied Health
Nuclear Medicine Tech.
    Program
129 Longwood Ave.
Boston, MA 02215

Salem State College
Nuclear Medicine Tech.
    Program
352 Lafayette St.
Salem, MA 01970

Springfield Technical
    Community College
Nuclear Medicine Tech.
    Program
One Armory Sq.
Springfield, MA 01105

University of Massachusetts
    Medical Center/Worcester
    State College
University of Massachusetts
    Medical Center
Nuclear Medicine Tech.
    Program
55 Lake Ave. North
Worcester, MA 06655

Michigan

Ferris State University
Nuclear Medicine Tech.
Program
901 S. State St. VFS 411
Big Rapids, MI 49307

William Beaumont
Hospital
Nuclear Medicine Tech.
Program
3601 W. Thirteen Mile Rd.
Royal Oak, MI 48073

Minnesota

Mayo Foundation
School of Health Related
Sciences
Nuclear Medicine Tech.
Program
1106 Siebens
Rochester, MN 55905

St. Mary's College
Nuclear Medicine Tech.
Program
700 Terrace Heights,
P.O. Box 10
Winona, MN 55987-1399

Mississippi

University of Mississippi
Medical Center
Nuclear Medicine Tech.
Program
2500 N. State St.
Jackson, MS 39216

Missouri

Research Medical Center
Nuclear Medicine Tech.
Program
2316 E. Meyer Blvd.
Kansas City, MO 64132

VA Medical Center
Nuclear Medicine Program-
115 J.C.
St. Louis, MO 63106

University of Missouri—Columbia
Nuclear Medicine Tech.
Program
504 Lewis Hall
Columbia, MO 65203

Nebraska

University of Nebraska
Medical Center
Nuclear Medicine Tech.
Program
600 S. Forty-second St.
Omaha, NE 68198-1045

Nevada

University of Nevada
Nuclear Medicine Tech.
Program
4505 Maryland Pkwy.
Las Vegas, NV 89154

New Jersey

Gloucester County College
Nuclear Medicine Tech.
Program
1400 Tanyard Rd.
Sewell, NJ 08080

Muhlenberg Regional
  Medical Center
  Nuclear Medicine Tech.
  Program
Park Ave. & Randolph Rd.
Plainfield, NJ 07061

Riverview Medical Center
  Nuclear Medicine Tech.
  Program
One Riverview Plaza
Red Bank, NJ 07701

University of Medicine and
  Dentistry of New Jersey
School of Health Related
  Professions
Nuclear Medicine Tech.
  Program, Room 321
65 Bergen St.
Newark, NJ 07107

New Mexico

University of New Mexico
  School of Medicine
Nuclear Medicine Tech.
  Program
Health Sciences and Service
  Building, Room 214
Albuquerque, NM 87131

New York

CUNY Bronx Community
  College
Nuclear Medicine Tech.
  Program
Montefiora Medical Center
111 E. 210th St.
Bronx, NY 10467

Institute of Allied Medical
  Professions
Nuclear Medicine Tech.
  Program
405 Parr Ave., Suite 501
New York, NY 10022

Manhattan College
Nuclear Medicine Tech.
  Program
Manhattan College Pkwy.
Riverdale, NY 10471

Molloy College
Nuclear Medicine Tech.
  Program
1000 Hempstead Ave.
P.O. Box 5002
Rockville Center, NY
  11571-5002

New York University Medical
  Center
Nuclear Medicine Tech.
  Program
Division of Nuclear Medicine
560 Fifth Ave.
New York, NY 10016

Rochester Institute of Technology
Nuclear Medicine Tech.
  Program
85 Lomb Memorial Dr.
Rochester, NY 14623

St. Vincent's Hospital and
  Medical Center
  of New York
Nuclear Medicine Tech.
  Program
153 W. Eleventh St.
New York, NY 10011

St. Vincent's Medical Center
of Richmond
Nuclear Medicine Tech.
Program
355 Bard Ave.
Staten Island, NY 10310

SUNY Health Science Center
at Buffalo
Nuclear Medicine Tech.
Program
105 Parker Hall
Buffalo, NY 14214

Veterans Administration
Medical Center
Nuclear Medicine Tech.
Program
79 Middleville Rd.
Northport, NY 11768

North Carolina

Caldwell Community College
and Technical Institute
Nuclear Medicine Program
2855 Hickory Blvd.
Hudson, NC 28638

Forsyth Technical Community
College
Nuclear Medicine Tech.
Program
2100 Silas Creek Pkwy.
Winston-Salem, NC 27103

Pitt Community College
Nuclear Medicine Tech.
Program
P.O. Drawer 7007
Greenville, NC 27835-7007

University of North Carolina
Hospitals
Nuclear Medicine Tech.
Program
101 Manning Dr.
Chapel Hill, NC 27514

Ohio

Aultman Hospital
Nuclear Medicine Tech.
Program
2600 Sixth St. SW
Canton, OH 44710

Ohio State University Hospitals
Nuclear Medicine Tech.
Program
410 W. Tenth Ave.
Doam Hall, Room 203E
Columbus, OH 43210

St. Elizabeth Hospital
Medical Center
Nuclear Medicine Tech.
Program
1044 Belmont Ave.
Youngstown, OH 44501

University of Cincinnati
Medical Center
Nuclear Medicine Tech.
Program
ML 0577
Cincinnati, OH 45267

The University of Findlay
Nuclear Medicine Tech.
Program
1000 N. Main St.
Findlay, OH 45840

Oklahoma

University of Oklahoma
  at Oklahoma City
  Nuclear Medicine Tech.
  Program
  P.O. Box 26901
  Oklahoma City, OK 73190

Oregon

Veterans Administration Medical
  Center/Portland
  Nuclear Medicine Tech.
  Program (115)
  P.O. Box 1034
  Portland, OR 97207

Pennsylvania

Cedar Crest College
  Nuclear Medicine Tech.
  Program
  100 College Dr.
  Biology 6622
  Allentown, PA 18104-6196

Community College
  of Allegheny City—
  Allegheny Campus
  Nuclear Medicine Tech.
  Program
  808 Ridge Ave.
  Pittsburgh, PA 15212

Lancaster Institute for Health
  Education
  Nuclear Medicine Tech.
  Program
  P.O. Box 3555
  Lancaster, PA 17604-3555

Wyoming Valley Health Care
  System, Inc.
  Nuclear Medicine Tech.
  Program
  575 N. River St.
  Wilkes-Barre, PA 18764

Puerto Rico

University of Puerto Rico
  Nuclear Medicine Tech.
  Program
  Medical Sciences Campus
  P.O. Box 365067
  San Juan, PR 00936

Rhode Island

Rhode Island Hospital
  Nuclear Medicine Tech.
  Program
  593 Eddy St.
  Providence, RI 02902

South Carolina

Midlands Technical
  College
  Nuclear Medicine Tech.
  Program
  P.O. Box 2408
  Columbia, SC 29202

South Dakota

Southeast Vocational
  Technical Institute
  Program Director
  2301 Career Pl.
  Sioux Falls, SD 57107

Tennessee

Baptist Memorial Hospital
Nuclear Medicine Tech.
Program
899 Madison Ave.
Memphis, TN 38146

Chattanooga State Community
College
Nuclear Medicine Tech.
Program
Department of Allied Health
4501 Amnicola Hwy.
Chattanooga, TN 37406

Methodist Hospitals
of Memphis
School of Nuclear Medicine
Technology
1265 Union Ave.
Memphis, TN 38104

University of Tennessee
Medical Center
at Knoxville
Nuclear Medicine Tech.
Program
1924 Alcoa Hwy.
Knoxville, TN 37920

Vanderbilt University
Medical Center
Radiology Department—
CCC-1124—Medical
Center North
Nuclear Medicine Tech.
Program
Twenty-first and Garland
Nashville, TN 37232-2675

Texas

Amarillo College
Nuclear Medicine Department
P.O. Box 447
Amarillo, TX 79178

Baylor College of Medicine
Nuclear Medicine Tech.
Program
Center for Allied Health
Sciences
One Baylor Plaza
Houston, TX 77030

Galveston College/University
of Texas
Nuclear Medicine Tech.
Program
4015 Avenue Q
Galveston, TX 77550

Houston Community College
System
Nuclear Medicine Tech.
Program
3100 Shenandoah
Houston, TX 77021

Incarnate Word College
Nuclear Medicine Tech.
Program
4301 Broadway
San Antonio, TX 78209

Utah

University of Utah Health
Sciences Center
Nuclear Medicine Tech.
Program
50 N. Medical Dr.
Salt Lake City, UT 84132

Weber State University
Nuclear Medicine Tech.
Program
3925 University Circle
Ogden, UT 84408-1602

Vermont

University of Vermont
Nuclear Medicine Tech.
Program
Rowell Building, Room 30
Burlington, VT 05405

Virginia

Medical College of Virginia/
Virginia Commonwealth
University
Department of Radiation
Sciences
Nuclear Medicine Tech.
Program
MVC Campus,
Box 980495
Richmond, VA
23298-0495

Old Dominion University
Nuclear Medicine Tech.
Program
209 Science Bldg.
Norfolk, VA 23529

University of Virginia
Medical Center
School of Nuclear Medicine
Technology
Box 486
Charlottesville, VA 22908

Washington

Virginia Mason Medical Center
Nuclear Medicine, H5-NU
P.O. Box 900
Seattle, WA 98111

West Virginia

West Virginia State College
Nuclear Medicine Tech.
Program
Campus Box 183, Box 1000
Institute, WV 25112

West Virginia University Hospital
Nuclear Medicine Tech.
Program
P.O. Box 8062
Morgantown WV 26506

Wheeling Jesuit College
Nuclear Medicine Tech.
Program
316 Washington Ave.
Wheeling, WV 26003

Wisconsin

Froedtert Memorial Lutheran
Hospital
Nuclear Medicine Tech.
Program
9200 W. Wisconsin Ave.
Milwaukee, WI 53226

Gundersen Med. Foundation/
LaCrosse Lutheran Hospital
Gundersen Clinic, Ltd.
Nuclear Medicine Tech.
Internship Program
1836 South Ave.
LaCrosse, WI 54601

St. Joseph's Hospital
Nuclear Medicine Tech.
Program
611 St. Joseph Ave.
Marshfield, WI 54449

St. Luke's Medical Center
Nuclear Medicine Tech.
Program
2900 W. Oklahoma Ave.
Milwaukee, WI 53215

Canada
Southern Alberta Institute
of Technology
Nuclear Medicine Tech.
Program
1301 Sixteenth Ave., NW
Calgary, Alberta
Canada T2M 0L4

British Columbia Institute
of Technology
Nuclear Medicine Tech.
Program
3700 Willingdon Ave.
Burnaby, British Columbia
Canada, V5G 3H2

Saint John Regional Hospital
Nuclear Medicine Training
Program
P.O. Box 2100 Stn. Main
Saint John, New Brunswick
Canada E2L 4L2

NSCC-Institute of Technology
Campus
Division of Nuclear Medicine
5685 Leeds St.
P.O. Box 2210 Stn. General
Halifax, Nova Scotia
Canada B3J 3C4

Michener Institute for Applied
Health Sciences
Nuclear Medicine Tech.
Program
222 St. Patrick St.
Toronto, Ontario
Canada M5T 1V4

APPENDIX D

ACCREDITED RADIOLOGIC TECHNOLOGIST (RADIOGRAPHER) PROGRAMS

The following are programs accredited by a mechanism acceptable to the ARRT.

Alabama

School of Radiography
Carraway Methodist
Medical Center
1615 Twenty-fifth St. North
Birmingham, AL
35234

School of Radiography
Jefferson State Community
College
2601 Carson Rd.
Birmingham, AL 35215

School of Radiography
University of Alabama
at Birmingham
1714 Ninth Ave. S.,
Room 354
Birmingham, AL
35294-1270

School of Radiography
Geo. Wallace State Community
College
Route #6, Box 62
Dothan, AL 36303

School of Radiography
Gadsden State Community
College
1001 Wallace Dr.
P.O. Box 227
Gadsden, AL 35902-0227

School of Radiography
Wallace State College
P.O. Box 2000
Hanceville, AL 35077-2000

School of Radiography
Huntsville Hospital
101 Sivley Rd.
Huntsville, AL 35801

School of Radiography
University of South Alabama-
Springhill Campus
1504 Springhill Ave., #2515
Mobile, AL 36604-3273

School of Radiography
Baptist Medical Center
2190 E. South Blvd.
Montgomery, AL 36116

School of Radiography
Southern Union State
Community College
1701 Lafayette Pkwy.
Opelika, AL 36801

School of Radiography
DCH Regional Medical Center
809 University Blvd. East
Tuscaloosa, AL 35401

Arizona

School of Radiologic Technology
Pima Medical Institute
957 S. Dobson Rd.
Mesa, AZ 85202

School of Radiography
Apollo College Inc.
2701 W. Bethany Home Rd.
Phoenix, AZ 85017

School of Radiography
Gateway Community College
108 N. Fortieth St.
Phoenix, AZ 85034

School of Radiography
Pima County Community
College
2202 W. Anklam Rd., HRP 220
Tucson, AZ 85709-0080

School of Radiologic Technology
Pima Medical Institute
3350 E. Grant Rd.
Tucson, AZ 85716

Arkansas

School of Radiography
South Arkansas Community
College
P.O. Box 7010/
300 Southwest Ave.
El Dorado, AR 71731-7010

School of Radiography
University of Arkansas for
Med Science AHEC-NW
2907 East Joyce St.
Fayetteville, AR 72703

School of Radiography
St. Edward Mercy
Medical Center
7301 Rogers Ave.,
Box 17000
Fort Smith, AR 72917

School of Radiography
Sparks Regional
Medical Center
Box 17006
Fort Smith, AR 72917

School of Radiography
North Arkansas
College
1515 Pioneer Dr.
Harrison, AR 72601

School of Radiography
Garland County Community
College
101 College Dr.
Hot Springs, AR 71913

School of Radiography
Baptist Medical System
11900 Colonel Glenn,
Suite 1000
Little Rock, AR 72210

School of Radiography
St. Vincent Infirmary
Medical Center
Two St. Vincent Circle
Little Rock, AR 72205

School of Radiography
University of Arkansas
for Medical Science
4301 W. Markham,
Slot 563
Little Rock, AR 72205

School of Radiography
Jefferson Regional
Medical Center
1515 W. Forty-second Ave.
Pine Bluff, AR 71603

School of Radiography
Arkansas State University
College of Nursing & Health
Professions/Box 910
State University, AR 72467

School of Radiography
University of Arkansas for
Medical Sciences
300 E. Sixth St.,
AHEC-Southwest
Texarkana, AR 71854

California

School of Radiography
Cabrillo College
6500 Soquel Dr.
Aptos, CA 95003

School of Radiography
Bakersfield College
1801 Panorama Drive
Bakersfield, CA 93305

School of Radiography
Mills-Peninsula
Hospitals
1783 El Camino Real
Burlingame, CA 94010

School of Radiography
Arrowhead Reginal
Medical Center
400 N. Pepper
Colton, CA 92324-1817

School of Radiography
Orange Coast College
2701 Fairview Rd.
P.O. Box 5005
Costa Mesa, CA
92628-5005

School of Radiography
Cypress College
9200 Valley View St.
Cypress, CA 90630

School of Radiography
Fresno City College
1101 E. University Ave.
Fresno, CA 93741

School of Radiography
Daniel Freeman Memorial
Hospital
333 N. Prairie Ave.
Inglewood, CA 90301

School of Radiography
Loma Linda University
SAHP/ Nichol Hall A-829
Loma Linda, CA 92350

School of Radiography
Long Beach City College
4901 E. Carson St.
Long Beach, CA 90808

School of Radiography
Foothill Community
College
12345 El Monte Rd.
Los Altos Hills, CA 94022

School of Radiography
Chas. Drew University
of Medicine & Science
1621 E. 120th St.
Los Angeles, CA 90059

School of Radiography
Childrens Hospital
4650 Sunset Blvd.
P.O. Box 54700
Los Angeles, CA 90027

School of Radiography
Los Angeles City College
855 N. Vermont Ave.
Los Angeles, CA 90029

School of Radiography
Yuba Community College
2088 N. Beale Rd.
Marysville, CA 95901

School of Radiography
Merced College
3600 "M" St.
Merced, CA
95348-2898

School of Radiography
Moorpark College
7075 Campus Rd.
Moorpark, CA 93060

School of Radiography
California State University-
Northridge
18111 Nordhoff St./
Health Sciences
Northridge, CA 91330-8285

School of Radiography
Merritt College
12500 Campus Dr.
Oakland, CA 94619

School of Radiography
St. John's Regional
Medical Center
1600 N. Rose Ave.
Oxnard, CA 93030

School of Radiography
Huntington Memorial Hospital
100 W. California Blvd.
Pasadena, CA 91109-7013

School of Radiography
Pasadena City College
1570 E. Colorado Blvd.
Pasadena, CA 91106-2003

School of Radiography
Chaffey College
5885 Haven Ave./ PLHS School
Rancho Cucamonga, CA 91737

School of Radiography
Canada College
4200 Farm Hill Blvd.
Redwood City, CA 94061

School of Radiography
Kaiser Permanente
Richmond MC
901 Nevin Ave.
Richmond, CA 94801

Advanced X-Ray Technician
   School
   Naval School Health Sciences
   34101 Farenholt Ave.
   San Diego, CA 92134-5219

School of Radiography
   San Diego Mesa College
   7250 Mesa College Dr.
   San Diego, CA 92111

School of Radiography
   City College
   of San Francisco
   50 Phelan Ave.
   San Francisco, CA 94112

School of Radiography
   Santa Barbara City College
   721 Cliff Dr.
   Santa Barbara, CA 93109

School of Radiography
   Santa Rosa Junior College
   1501 Mendocino Ave.
   Santa Rosa, CA 95401

School of Radiography
   San Joaquin
   General Hospital
   P.O. Box 1020
   Stockton, CA 95201

School of Radiography
   Olive View-UCLA
   Medical Center
   14445 Olive View Dr.
   Sylmar, CA 91342

School of Radiography
   El Camino College
   16007 S. Crenshaw Blvd.
   Torrance, CA 90506

School of Radiography
   La County Harbor/UCLA
   Medical Center
   1000 W. Carson St., Box 27
   Torrance, CA 90509

School of Radiography
   Mount San Antonio
   Community College
   1100 N. Grand Ave.
   Walnut, CA
   91789-1399

Colorado

School of Radiography
   Memorial Hospital
   2790 N. Academy Blvd.,
   Suite 201
   Colorado Springs, CO 80917

School of Radiography
   Community College
   of Denver
   P.O. Box 173363
   Denver, CO 80217-3363

School of Radiography
   Concorde Career Insitute
   770 Grant
   Denver, CO 80203

School of Radiography
   Pima Medical Institute
   1701 W. Seventy-second Ave.
   Denver, CO 80221

School of Radiography
   St. Anthony Hospital-
   Centura Health
   1601 N. Lowell Blvd.
   Denver, CO 80204

School of Radiography
Mesa State College
P.O. Box 2647,
    Dept. Nursing/Rad. Sci.
Grand Junction, CO
    81502

School of Radiography
Aims Community
    College
5401 W. Twentieth St.
P.O. Box 69
Greeley, CO 80632

School of Radiography
Red Rocks Community
    College
13300 W. Sixth Ave.
Lakewood, CO
    80228-1255

School of Radiography
Pueblo Community
    College
900 W. Orman Ave.
Pueblo, CO 81004

Connecticut

School of Radiography
St. Vincent's
    College
2800 Main St.
Bridgeport, CT 06606

School of Radiography
Danbury Hospital
24 Hospital Ave.
Danbury, CT 06810

School of Radiography
Quinnipiac College
Mount Carmel Ave.
Hamden, CT 06518

School of Radiography
Capital Community-
    Technical College
61 Woodland St.
Hartford, CT 06105

School of Radiography
Hartford Hospital
560 Hudson St.
Hartford, CT 06106

School of Radiography
Middlesex Community College
100 Training Hill Rd.
Middletown, CT 06457

School of Radiography
Gateway Community
    Technical College
88 Bassett Rd.
North Haven, CT 06473

School of Radiography
Stamford Hospital
Shelburne Rd. at W. Broad St.
Stamford, CT 06902

School of Radiography
Naugatuck Valley Community-
    Technical College
750 Chase Pkwy.
Waterbury, CT 06708

School of Radiography
University of Hartford
200 Bloomfield Ave.,
    Dana Hall 232
West Hartford, CT 06117

School of Radiography
Windham Community
    Memorial Hospital
112 Mansfield Ave.
Willimantic, CT 06226

Delaware

School of Radiography
    Delaware Technical &
    Community College
    P.O. Box 610
    Southern Campus
    Georgetown, DE 19947

School of Radiography
    Delaware Technical
    & Community College
    333 Shipley St.
    Wilmington, DE 19801

District of Columbia

Melva Boatright (Med-537)
    Bureau of Medicine & Surgery
    2300 "E" St. NW
    Washington, DC 20372-5300

School of Radiography
    University of the District
    of Columbia
    4200 Connecticut Ave. NW
    Washington, DC 20008

School of Radiography
    Washington Hospital Center
    110 Irving St. NW
    Washington, DC 20010

Florida

School of Radiography
    West Boca Medical Center
    21644 State Rd. 7
    Boca Raton, FL 33428

School of Radiography
    Bethesda Memorial
    Hospital Inc.
    2815 S. Seacrest Blvd.
    Boynton Beach, FL 33435

School of Radiography
    Manatee Community College
    P.O. Box 1849
    Bradenton, FL 34206

School of Radiography
    Brevard Community
    College
    1519 Clearlake Rd.
    Cocoa, FL 32934

School of Radiography
    Broward Community
    College
    3501 SW. Davie Rd.
    Davie, FL 33314

School of Radiography
    Halifax Medical Center
    303 N. Clyde Morris
    P.O. Box 2830
    Daytona Beach, FL 32120

School of Radiography
    Keiser College
    1500 NW. Forty-ninth St.
    Ft. Lauderdale, FL 33309

School of Radiography
    Edison Community College
    8099 College Pkwy. SW
    P.O. Box 60210
    Fort Myers, FL 33906-6210

School of Radiography
    Indian River Community
    College
    3209 Virginia Ave.
    Fort Pierce, FL 34981-5599

School of Radiography
    Santa Fe Community College
    3000 NW. Eighty-third St.
    Gainesville, FL 32606-6200

School of Radiography
Baptist/St. Vincent's
    Medical Center
1800 Barrs St./ P.O. Box 2982
Jacksonville, FL 32204

School of Radiography
University Medical Center
655 W. Eighth St.
Jacksonville, FL 32209

School of Radiography
Lakeland General Hospital
1324 Lakeland Hills Blvd.
    95448
Lakeland, FL 33804

School of Radiography
Jackson Memorial Medical
    Center/University
    of Miami
1611 NW. Twelfth Ave.
Miami, FL 33136

School of Radiography
Miami-Dade Community
    College
950 NW. Twentieth St.
Miami, FL 33127

School of Radiography
Mt. Sinai Medical Center
    Greater Miami
4300 Alton Rd.
Miami Beach, FL 33140

School of Radiography
Pasco-Hernandez Community
    College
10230 Ridge Rd.
New Port Richey, FL
    34654-5199

School of Radiologic Technology
Marion County School
    of Radiologic Technology
1014 SW. Seventh Rd.
Ocala, FL 34474

School of Radiography
Florida Hospital College
    of Health Science
800 Lake Estelle Dr.
Orlando, FL 32803

School of Radiography
University of Central Florida/
    Health and Physics
4000 Central Florida Blvd.,
    Room 102
Orlando, FL 32816-2220

School of Radiography
Valencia Community College
P.O. Box 3028, Mail Code 4-14
Orlando, FL 32802

School of Radiography
Palm Beach Community
    College
3160 PGA Boulevard
Palm Beach Gardens, FL
    33410

School of Radiologic Technology
Gulf Coast Community
    College
5239 W. US Hwy. 98
Panama City, FL 32401-1041

School of Radiography
Pensacola Junior College
5555 W. Hwy. 98/
    Applied Health
Pensacola, FL 32507-1097

School of Radiologic Technology
St. Petersburg Junior
College
P.O. Box 13489
St. Petersburg, FL 33733

School of Radiography
Hillsborough Community
College
P.O. Box 30030
Tampa, FL 33630

School of Radiography
Polk Community College
999 Ave. H NW
Winter Haven, FL 33881

Georgia

School of Radiography
Albany Technical
Institute
1021 Lowe Rd.
Albany, GA 31708

School of Radiography
Athens Area Technical
Institute
800 US Hwy. 29 N
Athens, GA 30601-1500

School of Radiography
Atlanta Medical Center
303 Pkwy., Box 51
Atlanta, GA 30312

School of Radiography
Emory University School
of Medicine
1364 Clifton Rd. NE,
Room BGO7
Atlanta, GA 30322

School of Radiography
Grady Health System
80 Butler St. SE/Box 26095
Atlanta, GA 30335

School of Radiography
Medical College of Georgia
Dept. of Radiography
Technology AE1003
Augusta, GA 30912-0600

School of Radiography
University Hospital
1350 Walton Way
Augusta, GA 30910

School of Radiography
Coastal Georgia State
College
3700 Altama Ave.
Brunswick, GA
31520-3644

School of Radiography
Carroll Technical Institute
997 S. Hwy. 16
Carrollton, GA 30116

School of Radiography
Medical Center Inc.
P.O. Box 951,
1951 Eighth Ave.
Columbus, GA 31994

School of Radiography
Dalton College
313 N. College Dr.
Dalton, GA 00003-0720

School of Radiography
De Kalb Medical Center
2701 N. Decatur Rd.
Decatur, GA 30033

School of Radiography
    Heart of Georgia Technical
        Institute
    560 Pine Hill Rd.
    Dublin, GA 31021-8896

School of Radiography
    Griffin Technical Institute
    501 Varsity Rd.
    Griffin, GA 30223-2042

School of Radiography
    West Georgia Technical
        Institute
    303 Fort Dr.
    Lagrange, GA 30240

School of Radiography
    Gwinnett Tech
    5150 Sugarloaf Pkwy.
    P.O. Box 1505
    Lawrenceville, GA 30246

School of Radiography
    Medical Center of Central
        Georgia
    777 Hemlock St. Hosp.
        Box #120
    Macon, GA 31208

Wellstar Kennestone Radiography
        Program
    Wellstar Medical Imaging
        Dept.
    60 Lacy St.
    Marietta, GA 30060

School of Radiography
    Moultrie Area Technology
        Institute
    361 Industrial Dr.
    Moultrie, GA 31768

School of Radiography
    Coosa Valley Technical
        Institute
    785 Cedar Ave.
    Rome, GA 30161

School of Radiography
    Armstrong Atlantic State
        University
    11935 Abercorn
    Savannah, GA 31419

School of Radiography
    Ogeechee Technical
        Institute
    1 Joe Kennedy Blvd.
    Statesboro, GA 30458

School of Radiography
    Thomas Technical
        Institute
    15689 US Hwy. 19N
    Thomasville, GA 31792

School of Radiography
    Valdosta Technical Institute
    P.O. Box 928 Val-Tech Rd.
    Valdosta, GA 31603

School of Radiography
    Middle Georgia
        Technical Institute
    80 Cohen Walker Dr.
    Warner Robins, GA 31088

School of Radiography
    Okefenokee Technical
        Institute
    1701 Carswell Ave.
    Waycross, GA 31503

Hawaii

School of Radiography
University of Hawaii/Kapiolani
Community College
4303 Diamond Head Rd./
Hlth. Sci.
Honolulu, HI 96816

Idaho

School of Radiography
Boise State University
1910 University Dr.
Boise, ID 83725

School of Radiography
Idaho State University
Box 8002
Pocatello, ID 83209

Illinois

School of Radiography
Northwest Community
Hospital
800 W. Central Rd.
Arlington Heights, IL
60005

School of Radiography
Belleville Area College
2500 Carlyle Ave.
Belleville, IL
62221-5899

School of Radiography
Southern Illinois University
at Carbondale
College of Applied Science
& Arts
Carbondale, IL 62901

School of Radiography
Kaskaskia College
27210 College Rd.
Centralia, IL 62801

School of Radiography
Parkland College
2400 W. Bradley Ave.
Champaign, IL 61821

School of Radiography
Cook County Hospital
1825 W. Harrison St.
Chicago, IL 60612

School of Radiography
Malcolm X Community
College
1900 W. Van Buren Ave.
Chicago, IL 60612

School of Radiography
Ravenswood Hospital
Medical Center
4550 N. Winchester Ave.
Chicago, IL 60640

School of Radiography
Trinity Hospital
2320 E. Ninety-third St.
Chicago, IL 60617

School of Radiography
Wilbur Wright College
4300 N. Narragansett
Chicago, IL 60634

School of Radiography
Provena United
Sameritans MC
812 N. Logan Ave.
(Logan Campus)
Danville, IL 61832

School of Radiography
Sauk Valley College
173 Illinois, Route #2
Dixon, IL 61021-9110

School of Radiography
St. Francis Hospital
355 Ridge Ave.
Evanston, IL 60202

School of Radiography
Carl Sandburg Junior
College
2232 S. Lake Storey Rd.
Galesburg, IL 61401

School of Radiography
College of Du Page
425 N. Twenty-second St.
Glen Ellyn, IL 60137

School of Radiography
College of Lake County
19351 W. Washington St.
Grayslake, IL 60030

School of Radiography
Kankakee Community
College
P.O. Box 888, River Rd.
Kankakee, IL
60901-0888

School of Radiography
McDonough District
Hospital
525 E. Grant St.
Macomb, IL 61455

School of Radiography
Kishwaukee College
21193 Malta Rd.
Malta, IL 60150

School of Radiography
Trinity Medical Center-
East Campus
555 Sixth St.
Moline, IL
61265-1216

Bloomington-Normal School
of Radiography
Bromen Healthcare
900 Franklin Ave.
Normal, IL 61761

School of Radiography
Olney Central College
5 RMH 800 E. Locust St.
Olney, IL 62450

School of Radiography
Moraine Valley Community
College
10900 S. Eighty-eighth Ave.,
#B-130
Palos Hills, IL 60465

School of Radiography
Illinois Central College
201 SW Adams
Peoria, IL
61635-0001

School of Radiography
St. Francis Medical Center
530 NE Glen Oak Ave.
Peoria, IL 61637

School of Radiography
Blessing Hospital
P.O. Box 7005/
Broadway at Fourteenth
Quincy, IL
62301-7005

School of Radiography
Triton College
2000 N. Fifth Ave.
River Grove, IL 60171

School of Radiography
Rockford Memorial
Hospital
2400 N. Rockton Ave.
Rockford, IL 61101

School of Radiography
Swedish-American
Hospital
1400 Charles St.
Rockford, IL 61101

School of Radiography
South Suburban College
of Cook County
15800 S. State St.
South Holland, IL 60473

School of Radiography
Lincolnland Community
College
Shepherd Rd.
Springfield, IL
62794-9256

Indiana

School of Radiography
Columbus Regional Hospital
2400 E. Seventeenth St.
Columbus, IN 47201

School of Radiography
University of Southern
Indiana
8600 University Blvd.
Evansville, IN 47712

School of Radiography
Welborn Memorial Baptist
Hospital
401 SE Sixth St.
Evansville, IN 47713

Fort Wayne School
of Radiography
Parkview Memorial/St. Joseph
Medical Center
700 Broadway Ave.
Fort Wayne, IN 46802

School of Radiography
University of St. Francis
3024 Fairfield Ave.
Fort Wayne, IN 46807

School of Radiography
Indiana University
Northwest
3400 Broadway
Gary, IN 46408

School of Radiography
Hancock Memorial Hospital
and Health Services
801 N. State St.
Greenfield, IN 46140

School of Radiography
Ball State University/Allied
Health Education
I 65 & Twenty-first St.
Indianapolis, IN
46206-1367

School of Radiography
Community Hospitals
of Indianapolis
1500 N. Ritter Ave.
Indianapolis, IN 46219

School of Radiography
Indiana University School
of Medicine
541 Clinical Dr., #120
Indianapolis, IN 46202-5111

School of Radiography
Ivy Tech State College
1 W. Twenty-sixth St.,
P.O. Box 1763
Indianapolis, IN 46206

School of Radiography
St. Joseph Hospital
and Health Center
1907 W. Sycamore St.
Kokomo, IN 46901

School of Radiography
The King's Daughter's
Hospital
One King's Daughter's Dr.,
P.O. Box 447
Madison, IN 47250

School of Radiography
Ball Memorial Hospital
2401 University Ave.
Muncie, IN 47303

School of Radiography
Reid Hospital and Health Care
Services
1401 Chester Blvd.
Richmond, IN 47374

School of Radiography
Indiana University
at South Bend
1700 Mishawaka Ave.
P.O. Box 7111
South Bend, IN 46634-7111

School of Radiography
Ivy Tech State College
7999 US Hwy. 41 South
Terre Haute, IN 47802

School of Radiography
Porter Memorial Hospital
814 La Porte Ave.
Valparaiso, IN 46383

School of Radiography
The Good Samaritan Hospital
520 S. Seventh St.
Vincennes, IN 47591

Iowa

School of Radiography
Scott Community College
500 Belmont Rd.
Bettendorf, IA 52722-6804

School of Radiography
Mercy-St Luke's Hospital
1026 "A" Ave. NE
Cedar Rapids, IA 52402

School of Radiography
Jennie Edmunson Memorial
Hospital
933 E. Pierce St.
Council Bluffs, IA 51503

School of Radiography
Iowa Methodist Medical Center
1200 Pleasant St.
Des Moines, IA 50308

School of Radiography
Iowa Central Community
College
330 Ave. "M"
Fort Dodge, IA 50501

School of Radiography
  University of Iowa Hospital
    and Clinics
  Program in Radiologic Tech.
  Iowa City, IA 52242

School of Radiography
  North Iowa Mercy
    Health Center
  1000 Fourth St. SW
  Mason City, IA 50401

School of Radiography
  Indian Hills Community
    College
  525 Grandview
  Ottumwa, IA 52501

School of Radiography
  Northeast Iowa Community
    College
  10250 Sundown Rd.
  Peosta, IA 52068

School of Radiography
  St. Lukes Regional
    Medical Center
  2720 Stone Park Blvd.
  Sioux City, IA 51104

School of Radiography
  Allen College
  1825 Logan Ave.
  Waterloo, IA 50703

School of Radiography
  Covenant
    Medical Center
  3421 W. Ninth St.
  Waterloo, IA 50702

Kansas

School of Radiography
  Fort Hays State University
  600 Park St./
    Allied Health
  Hays, KS 67601-4099

School of Radiography
  Hutchinson Community
    College
  1300 N. Plum
  Hutchinson, KS 67501

School of Radiography
  Bethany Medical Center
  51 N. Twelfth St.
  Kansas City, KS 66102

School of Radiography
  Labette Community
    College
  200 S. Fourteenth St.
  Parsons, KS 67357

School of Radiography
  Washburn University
    of Topeka
  1700 SW College Avenue
  Topeka, KS 66621

School of Radiography
  Newman University
  3100 McCormick Ave.
  Wichita, KS 67213

Kentucky

School of Radiography
  King's Daughter's
    Medical Center
  2201 Lexington Ave.
  Ashland, KY 41101

School of Radiography
Bowling Green Technical
College
1845 Loop Dr.
Bowling Green, KY 42101

School of Radiography
Elizabethtown Technical
College
505 University Dr.
Elizabethtown, KY 42754

School of Radiography
Hazard Community College
Hwy 15 S., 1 Community
College Dr.
Hazard, KY 41701

School of Radiologic Technology
Northern Kentucky
University
Albright Health Center,
Room 227
Highland Heights, KY
41099-2104

School of Radiography
Central Kentucky Technical
College
308 Vo-Tech Rd.
Lexington, KY
40511-1020

School of Radiography
Lexington Community College
Oswald Building, Cooper Dr.
Lexington, KY 40506

School of Radiography
St. Joseph Hospital
One St. Joseph Dr.
Lexington, KY 40504

Radiologic Technology Program
University of Louisville/
School of Allied Health
555 S. Floyd/
K Bldg., HSC
Louisville, KY 40292

School of Radiography
Madisonville Technical
College
750 N. Laffoon St.
Madisonville, KY 42431

School of Radiography
Morehead State
University
UPO 784/408 Reed Hall
Morehead, KY 40351

School of Radiography
Owensboro Community
College
4800 New Hartford Rd.
Owensboro, KY 42303

School of Radiography
West Kentucky State
Technical School
5200 Blandville Rd.
P.O. Box 7408
Paducah, KY
42002-7408

School of Radiography
Cumberland Valley Technical
College
US 25E South,
P.O. Box 187
Pineville, KY 40977

Louisiana

School of Radiography
Baton Rouge General
Medical Center
3600 Florida Blvd.,
P.O. Box 2511
Baton Rouge, LA 70806

School of Radiography
Our Lady of the Lake College
5345 Brittany Dr.
Baton Rouge, LA 70808

School of Radiography
Louisiana State University
at Eunice
P.O. Box 1129/2048 Johnson
Eunice, LA 70535

School of Radiography
North Oaks Medical Center
P.O. Box 2668, Hwy. 51 South
Hammond, LA 70404

School of Radiography
Lafayette General
Medical Center
1214 Coolidge Ave.
P.O. Box 52009
Lafayette, LA 70505

School of Radiography
University Medical Center
2390 W. Congress
P.O. Box 69300
Lafayette, LA 70596-9300

School of Radiography
McNeese State University
P.O. Box 92000
Lake Charles, LA 70609

School of Radiography
Northeast Louisiana University
700 University Ave.
Monroe, LA 71201-0450

School of Radiography
Alton Ochsner Medical
Foundation
1516 Jefferson Hwy.
New Orleans, LA 70121

School of Radiography
Delgado Community College
615 City Park Ave.
New Orleans, LA 70119

School of Radiography
Northwestern State University
1800 Line Ave.
Shreveport, LA 71101

Radiologic Technology Program
Southern University-
Shreveport
3050 Martin Luther
King, Jr., Dr.
Shreveport, LA 71107

Maine

School of Radiography
Eastern Maine Technical
College
354 Hogan Rd.
Bangor, ME 04401

School of Radiography
Central Maine
Medical Center
300 Main St.
Lewiston, ME 04240

School of Radiography
Mercy Hospital
144 State St.
Portland, ME 04101

School of Radiologic Technology
Southern Maine Technical
College
2 Fort Rd.
South Portland, ME 04106

Maryland

School of Radiography
Anne Arundel Community
College
101 College Pkwy.,
Flrs 434
Arnold, MD 21012

School of Radiography
Essex Community College
7201 Rossville Blvd.
Baltimore, MD 21237

School of Radiography
Greater Baltimore
Medical Center
6701 N. Charles St.
Baltimore, MD 21204

School of Radiography
Johns Hopkins Hospital
600 N. Wolfe St.
Baltimore, MD 21205

School of Radiography
Maryland General
Hospital
827 Linden Ave.
Baltimore, MD 21201

School of Radiography
Allegany College of Maryland
12401 Willowbrook Rd. SE
Cumberland, MD 21502-2596

School of Radiography
Hagerstown Community
College
11400 Robinwood Dr.
Hagerstown, MD 21742

School of Radiography
Prince George's Community
College
301 Largo Rd./Allied Hlth. Dept.
Largo, MD 20774-2199

School of Radiography
Wor-Wic Community College
32000 Campus Dr.
Salisbury, MD 21804

School of Radiologic Technology
Holy Cross Hospital/
. Silver Spring
1500 Forest Glen Rd.
Silver Spring, MD 20910

School of Radiography
Montgomery College
7600 Takoma Ave.
Takoma Park, MD 20912

School of Radiography
Washington Adventist Hospital
7600 Carroll Ave.
Takoma Park, MD 20912

School of Radiography
Chesapeake College
P.O. Box 8
Wye Mills, MD 21679

Massachusetts

School of Radiography
Middlesex Community College
Springs Rd.
Bedford, MA 01730

School of Radiography
Bunker Hill Community
College
250 New Rutherford Ave.
B328P
Boston, MA 02129

School of Radiography
Massachusetts College of
Pharmacy and Allied Health
179 Longwood Ave.
Boston, MA 02115-5896

Radiography Program
Northeastern University
266 Ryder Hall/
360 Huntington Ave.
Boston, MA 02115

School of Radiography
Massasoit Community College
One Massasoit Blvd.
Brockton, MA 02402

School of Radiography
North Shore Community
College
1 Ferncroft Rd./P.O. Box 3340
Danvers, MA 01923-0840

School of Radiography
Northern Essex Community
College
100 Elliott Way
Haverhill, MA 01830

School of Radiography
Holyoke Community College
303 Homestead Ave.
Holyoke, MA 01040

School of Radiography
Springfield Technical
Community College
One Armory Square, Box 9000
Springfield, MA 01101-9000

School of Radiography
Massachusetts Bay
Community College
50 Oakland St.
Wellesley Hills, MA 02181

School of Radiography
Quinsigamond Community
College
670 W. Boylston St.
Worcester, MA 01606

Michigan

School of Radiography
Washtenaw Community
College
4800 E. Huron River Dr./P.O.
Box D-1
Ann Arbor, MI 48106-1610

School of Radiography
Kellogg Community College
450 North Ave.
Battle Creek, MI 49017

School of Radiography
Lake Michigan College
2755 E. Napier Ave.
Benton Harbor, MI 49022-1899

School of Radiography
Ferris State University
200 Ferris Dr.
Big Rapids, MI 49307

School of Radiography
Henry Ford Community
College
Main Campus, 5101
Evergreen Rd.
Dearborn, MI 48128-1495

School of Radiography
Grace Hospital
6071 W. Outer Dr.
Detroit, MI 48235

School of Radiography
Henry Ford Hospital
2799 W. Grand Blvd. WC 323-A
Detroit, MI 48202

School of Radiography
Marygrove College
8425 W. McNichols Rd.
Detroit, MI 48221

School of Radiography
St. John Hospital
and Medical Center
22101 Moross Rd.
Detroit, MI 48236

School of Radiography
Hurley Medical Center
One Hurley Plaza
Flint, MI 48502

School of Radiography
Grand Rapids Community
College
143 Bostwick Northeast
Grand Rapids, MI 49503

School of Radiography
Mid Michigan Community
College
1375 S. Clare Ave.
Harrison, MI 48625-9447

School of Radiography
Jackson Community College
2111 Emmons Rd.
Jackson, MI 49201

School of Radiologic Technology
Lansing Community College
419 N. Capital Ave.,
Box 40010
Lansing, MI 48901

School of Radiography
Marquette General Hospital
420 W. Magnetic St.
Marquette, MI 49855

School of Radiography
Baker College of Owosso
1020 S. Washington St.
Owosso, MI 48867-4400

School of Radiography
Port Huron Hospital
1001 Kearney St. P.O.
Box 5011
Port Huron, MI 48060

School of Radiography
William Beaumont Hospital
3601 W. 13 Mile Rd.
Royal Oak, MI 48072

School of Radiography
Oakland Community College
22322 Rutland Dr.
Southfield, MI 48075

School of Radiography
Providence Hospital
P.O. Box 2043-
16001 W. Nine Mile
Southfield, MI 48037

School of Radiography
Delta College
1961 Delta Dr.
University Center, MI 48710

School of Radiography
Oakwood-United
Hospitals Inc.
33155 Annapolis Rd.
Wayne, MI 48184

Minnesota

School of Radiography
Riverland Community
College
1900 Eighth Ave. NW
Austin, MN 55912

School of Radiography
Medical Institute
of Minnesota
5503 Green Valley Dr.
Bloomington, MN 55437

School of Radiography
Lake Superior College
2101 Trinity Rd.
Duluth, MN 55811

School of Radiologic Technology
Northwest Technical College-
East Grand Forks
2022 Central Ave. NE
East Grand Forks, MN
56721-2702

School of Radiography
The College of St. Catherine
601 Twenty-fifth Ave. South
Minneapolis, MN 55454

School of Radiography
Normandale Community
College
9700 France Ave.
Minneapolis, MN 55431

School of Radiography
Veterans Affairs
Medical Center
One Veterans Dr., #114
Minneapolis, MN 55417

School of X-Ray Technique
North Memorial
Medical Center
3300 Oakdale Ave. N
Robbinsdale, MN 55422

School of Radiography
Mayo Clinic/Mayo Foundation
200 First St. SW
Rochester, MN 55905

School of Radiography
St. Cloud Hospital
1406 Sixth Ave. North
St. Cloud, MN 56303

School of Radiography
Methodist Hospital
6500 Excelsior Blvd.
St. Louis Park, MN 55426

School of Radiography
Century Community and
Technical College
3300 Century Ave. North
White Bear Lake, MN 55110

School of Radiography
Rice Memorial Hospital
301 Becker Ave., SW
Willmar, MN 56201

Mississippi

School of Radiography
NE Mississippi Community
College
Cunningham Blvd.
Booneville, MS 38829

School of Radiography
Jones County Junior
College
900 Court St.
Ellisville, MS 39437

School of Radiography
Itawamba Community
College
602 W. Hill St.
Fulton, MS 38843

School of Radiography
Mississippi Gulf Coast
Community College
Jackson County Campus
P.O. Box 100
Gautier, MS 39553

School of Radiography
Forrest General Hospital
6051 US Hwy. 49
Hattiesburg, MS 39401

School of Radiography
Mississippi Baptist
Medical Center
1225 N. State St.
Jackson, MS 39201

School of Radiography
University of Mississippi
Medical Center
2500 N. State St.
Jackson, MS 39216

School of Radiography
Meridian Community
College
910 Highway 19 North
Meridian, MS 39307

School of Radiography
Mississippi Delta Community
College
Olive St./ P.O. Box 668
Moorhead, MS 38761

School of Radiography
Copiah-Lincoln Community
College
P.O. Box 649
Wesson, MS 39601-0649

Missouri

School of Radiography
University of Missouri-
Columbia
622 Lewis Hall
Columbia, MO 65211

School of Radiography
Sanford-Brown College
12006 Manchester Rd.
Des Peres, MO 63131

School of Radiography
Mineral Area Regional
Medical Center
1212 Weber Rd.
Farmington, MO 63640

School of Radiography
Nichols Career Center
609 Union
Jefferson City, MO 65101

School of Radiography
Missouri Southern State College
3950 Newman Rd.
Joplin, MO 64801

School of Radiography
Avila College
11901 Wornall Rd./
Nahsm Dept.
Kansas City, MO 64145

School of Radiography
Penn Valley Community
College
3201 SW Trafficway
Kansas City, MO 64111

School of Radiography
Research Medical Center
2316 E. Meyer Blvd.
Kansas City, MO 64132-1199

School of Radiography
North Kansas City Memorial
Hospital
2800 Clay Edwards Dr.
North Kansas City, MO 64116

School of Radiography
Sanford Brown College
of Kansas City
520 E. Nineteenth Ave.
North Kansas City, MO 64116

School of Radiography
Rolla Technical Center
500 Forum Dr.
Rolla, MO 65401

School of Radiography
Cox Health Systems
1423 N. Jefferson Ave.
Springfield, MO 65802

School of Radiography
St. John's Regional
Health Center
1235 E. Cherokee St.
Springfield, MO 65804

School of Radiography
Barnes Jewish Hospital
306 S. Kings Hwy.,
Suite 235
St Louis, MO 63110

School of Radiography
St. John's Mercy
Medical Center
615 S. New Ballas Rd.
St. Louis, MO 63141

School of Radiography
St. Louis Community College
at Forest Park
5600 Oakland Ave.
St. Louis, MO 63110

Montana

School of Radiography
St. Vincent Hospital
1233 N. Thirtieth St.,
Box 35200
Billings, MT 59107

School of Radiography
Benefis Healthcare
500 Fifteenth Ave. S,
Box 5013
Great Falls, MT 59405

School of Radiography
St. Patrick Hospital
500 W. Broadway,
P.O. Box 4587
Missoula, MT 59806

Nebraska

School of Radiography
Mary Lanning Memorial
Hospital
715 N. St. Joseph Ave.
Hastings, NE 68901

School of Radiography
Southeast Community
College
8800 "O" St.
Lincoln, NE 68520

School of Radiography
Alegent Health Immanuel
Medical Center
6901 N. Seventy-second St.
Omaha, NE
68122-1799

School of Radiography
Clarkson College
101 S. Forty-second St.
Omaha, NE 68131

School of Radiography
St. Joseph Hospital
601 N. Thirtieth St.
Omaha, NE 68131

School of Radiography
University of Nebraska
Medical Center
600 S. Forty-second St.
Omaha, NE 68198

School of Radiography
Regional West Medical Center
4021 N. Avenue B
Scottsbluff, NE 69381

Nevada

School of Radiography
University of Nevada- Las Vegas
4505 Maryland Pkwy.
Las Vegas, NV 89154-3017

School of Radiologic Technology
Truckee Meadows Community
College
7000 Dandini Blvd.
Reno, NV 89512

New Hampshire

School of Radiography
New Hampshire Tech Institute
11 Institute Dr.
Concord, NH 03301-7412

New Jersey

School of Radiography
Atlantic City Medical Center
1925 Pacific Ave.
Atlantic City, NJ 08401

School of Radiography
Hudson Area School of
Radiology Technology
29 E. Twenty-ninth St.
Bayonne, NJ 07002

School of Radiography
South Jersey Hospital System
Irving Ave. Bridgeton
Hosp. Div.
Bridgeton, NJ 08302

School of Radiography
Cooper Hospital University
Medical Center
One Cooper Plaza
Camden, NJ 08103

School of Radiography
West Jersey Hospital
Mt. Ephraim Lansdowne
Camden, NJ 08104

School of Radiography
Burdette Tomlin Memorial
Hospital
2 Stone Harbor Blvd.
Cape May Court House, NJ
08210

School of Radiography
Middlesex County College
2600 WoodbridgeAve.
P.O. Box 3050
Edison, NJ 08818-3050

School of Radiography
Englewood Hospital
and Medical Center
350 Engle St.
Englewood, NJ 07631

School of Radiography
Hackensack
Medical Center
30 Prospect Ave.,
Hillcrest Bldg.
Hackensack, NJ 07601

School of Radiography
Brookdale Community
College
765 Newman Springs Rd.
Lincroft, NJ 07738-1597

School of Radiography
Morristown Memorial
Hospital
100 Madison Ave.
Morristown, NJ 07962

School of Radiography
Essex County College
303 University Ave.
Newark, NJ 07102

School of Radiography
Bergen Community
College
400 Paramus Rd.
Paramus, NJ 07652

School of Radiography
Passaic County Community
College
One College Blvd.
Paterson, NJ 07505-1179

School of Radiography
Burlington County College
County Route 530
Pemberton, NJ 08068

School of Radiography
Muhlenberg Regional
Medical Center
Park Ave. & Randolph Rd.
Plainfield, NJ 07061

School of Radiography
Valley Hospital
223 N. Van Dien Ave.
Ridgewood, NJ 07450

School of Radiography
Shore Memorial Hospital
644 Shore Rd.
Somers Point, NJ 08244

School of Radiography
Helene Fuld Hospital
750 Brunswick Ave.
Trenton, NJ 08638

School of Radiography
Mercer County Community
College
P.O. Box B/Science
& Allied Health
Trenton, NJ 08690

School of Radiography
St. Francis Medical Center
601 Hamilton Ave.
Trenton, NJ 08629

School of Radiography
Cumberland County College
P.O. Box 517, College Dr.
Vineland, NJ 08360

School of Radiography
Pascack Valley Hospital
Old Hook Rd.
Westwood, NJ 07675

New Mexico

School of Radiography
Pima Medical Institute
2201 San Pedro NE,
Bldg. 3 # 100
Albuquerque, NM 87110

School of Radiologic Technology
University of New Mexico/
School of Medicine
Health Science Center/
Radiology Dept.
Albuquerque, NM
87131-5336

School of Radiography
Clovis Community College
417 Schepps Blvd.
Clovis, NM 88101

School of Medical Radiography
Northern New Mexico
Community College
1002 N. Onate St.
Espanola, NM 87532

School of Radiography
Dona Ana Branch Community
College
B 30001 Dept. 3DA/
3400 S. Espina
Las Cruces, NM
88003-8001

New York

School of Radiography
Broome Community College
P.O. Box 1017
Binghamton, NY 13902

School of Radiography
Bronx Community College
of CUNY
University Ave. & West 181 St.
Bronx, NY 10453

School of Radiography
Hostos Community College
475 Grand Concourse A-307
Bronx, NY 10451

School of Radiography
Long Island College
Hospital
340 Henry St.
Brooklyn, NY 11201

School of Radiography
Methodist Hospital-Bartone
506 Sixth St.
Brooklyn, NY 11215

School of Radiography
New York Technical College
of CUNY
300 Jay St.
Brooklyn, NY 11201

School of Radiography
SUNY Health Science Center
at Brooklyn
450 Clarkson Ave., Box 1226
Brooklyn, NY 11203

School of Radiography
Long Island University/CW
Post Campus
720 Northern Blvd.
Brookville, NY 11548-1300

School of Radiography
Trocaire Junior College
360 Choate Ave.
Buffalo, NY 14220-2094

School of Radiography
Arnot-Ogden Medical Center
Roe Ave.
Elmira, NY 14901

School of Radiography
Catholic Medical Center
175-05 H. Harding
Expressway
Fresh Meadows, NY 11365

School of Radiography
Nassau Community College
One Education Dr.
Garden City, NY 11530

School of Radiography
Glens Falls Hospital
100 Park St.
Glens Falls, NY 12801

School of Radiography
St. James Mercy Health
411 Canisteo St.
Hornell, NY 14843

School of Radiography
Women's Christian
Association Hospital
207 Foote Ave.
Jamestown, NY 14701

School of Radiography
Orange County Community
College
115 South St.
Middletown, NY 10940

School of Radiography
Winthrop-University
Hospital
259 First St.
Mineola, NY 11501

School of Radiography
Bellevue Hospital Center
1st Ave. & Twenty-seventh St.
New York, NY 10016

School of Radiography
Harlem Hospital Center
506 Lenox Ave., K Pavil.,
Rm. 415
New York, NY 10037

School of Radiography
Northport VA Medical Center
79 Middleville Rd. (632/153)
Northport, NY 11768

R. Hochstin School of Radiography
South Nassau Communities
Hospital
2445 Oceanside Rd.
Oceanside, NY 11572

School of Radiography
Champlain Valley
Physician's Hospital
75 Beekman St.
Plattsburgh, NY 12901

School of Radiography
United Hospital
406 Boston Post Rd.
Port Chester, NY 10573

School of Radiography
Central Suffolk Hospital
1300 Roanoke Ave.
Riverhead, NY 11901

School of Radiography
Monroe Community College
1000 E. Henrietta Rd.
Rochester, NY 14623-5780

School of Radiography
Mercy Medical Center
1000 N. Village Ave.
Rockville Centre, NY 11570

School of Radiography
Niagara County Community
College
3111 Saunders Settlement Rd.
Sanborn, NY 14132

School of Radiologic Technology
North Country Community
College
20 Winona Ave./P.O. Box 89
Saranac Lake, NY 12983

School of Radiography
SUNY Health Science Center
at Syracuse
750 E. Adams St.
Syracuse, NY 13210

School of Radiography
Hudson Valley Community
College
80 Vandenburgh Ave.
Troy, NY 12180

School of Radiography
St. Elizabeth Hospital
2209 Genesee St.
Utica, NY 13501

School of Radiography
St Luke's-Memorial
Hospital Center
Champlin Rd., P.O. Box 479
Utica, NY 13503

School of Radiography
Westchester Community
College
75 Grasslands Rd.
Valhalla, NY 10595-1698

North Carolina

School of Radiography
Asheville Buncombe Tech
Community College
340 Victoria Rd.
Asheville, NC 28806

School of Radiography
University of North Carolina
CB #7130 Wing E
Medical School
Chapel Hill, NC 27599-7130

School of Radiography
    Carolinas College of Health
        Science
    P.O. Box 32861/
        1200 Blythe Blvd.
    Charlotte, NC 28232-2861

School of Radiography
    Presbyterian Healthcare
    200 Hawthorne Ln.,
        P.O. Box 33549
    Charlotte, NC 28233

School of Radiography
    Fayetteville Technical
        Community College
    P.O. Box 35236
    Fayetteville, NC 28303

School of Radiography
    Moses H. Cone Memorial
        Hospital
    1200 N. Elm St.
    Greensboro, NC 27401

School of Radiography
    Pitt Community College
    Hwy. 11 South,
        P.O. Drawer 7007
    Greenville, NC 27835-7007

School of Radiography
    Vance-Granville Community
        College
    P.O. Box 917
    Henderson, NC 27536

School of Radiography
    Caldwell Community College
        and Technical Institute
    2855 Hickory Blvd.
    Hudson, NC 28638

School of Radiography
    Lenoir Memorial Hospital
    100 Airport Rd.
    P.O. Drawer 1678
    Kinston, NC 28501

School of Radiography
    Carteret Community
        College
    3505 Arendell St.
    Morehead City, NC
        28557-2989

School of Radiography
    Wilkes Regional Medical
        Center
    P.O. Box 609
    North Wilkesboro, NC
        28659

School of Radiography
    Sandhills Community College
    2200 Airport Rd.
    Pinehurst, NC 28374

School of Radiography
    Wake Technical Community
        College
    9101 Fayetteville Rd.
    Raleigh, NC 27603

School of Radiography
    Edgecombe Community
        College
    225 Tarboro St.
    Rocky Mount, NC 27801

School of Radiography
    Rowan-Cabarrus Community
        College
    P.O. Box 1595
    Salisbury, NC 28144

School of Radiography
Cleveland Community College
137 S. Post Rd.
Shelby, NC 28150

School of Radiography
Johnston Community College
P.O. Box 2350/ College Dr.
Smithfield, NC 27577

School of Radiography
Southwestern Community
College
275 Webster Rd.
Sylva, NC 28779

School of Radiography
Cape Fear Community College
411 N. Front St.
Wilmington, NC 28409

School of Radiography
Forsyth Technical Community
College
2100 Silas Creek Pkwy.
Winston-Salem, NC 27103

North Dakota

School of Radiography
Medcenter One Health
Systems
300 N. Seventh St.
Bismarck, ND 58506-5525

School of Radiography
St. Alexius Medical Center
900 E. Broadwat Ave.
Bismarck, ND 58506

School of Radiography
Merit Care Medical Center
720 Fourth St. North
Fargo, ND 58122

School of Radiography
Trinity Medical Center
One Burdick Exprswy. W,
P.O. Box 5020
Minot, ND 58701

Ohio

School of Radiography
Children's Hospital
Medical Center
One Perkins Sq.
Akron, OH 44308

School of Radiography
Columbia Mercy
Medical Center
1320 Mercy Dr. NW
Canton, OH 44708

School of Radiography
University of Cincinnati/
Raymond Walters College
234 Goodman/
Mail Location 579
Cincinnati, OH
45267-0579

School of Radiography
Xavier University
3800 Victory Pkwy.
Cincinnati, OH 45207-4331

School of Radiography
Columbus State Community
College
550 E. Spring St./
Union Hall 416
Columbus, OH 43215

School of Radiography
Ohio State University
1583 Perry St.
Columbus, OH 43210

School of Radiography
Sinclair Community College
444 W. Third St.
Dayton, OH 45402

School of Radiography
Lorain County Community
College
1005 N. Abbe Rd.
Elyria, OH 44035

School of Radiography
Meridia Euclid Hospital
18901 Lake Shore Blvd.
Euclid, OH 44119

School of Radiography
Kettering College
of Medical Arts
3737 Southern Blvd.
Kettering, OH 45429

School of Radiography
Lakeland Community
College
7700 Clocktower Dr.
Kirtland, OH 44094-5198

School of Radiography
Lima Technical College
4240 Campus Dr.
Lima, OH 45804

School of Radiography
North Central Technical
College
2441 Kenwood Cir.
Mansfield, OH 44905

School of Radiography
Marietta Memorial
Hospital
401 Mathews St.
Marietta, OH 45750

School of Radiography
Marion General Hospital
McKinley Park Dr.
Marion, OH 43302

School of Radiography
Middletown Regional
Hospital
105 McKnight Dr.
Middletown, OH 45044

School of Radiography
Central Ohio Technical
College
1179 University Dr.
Newark, OH 43055

School of Radiography
Cuyahoga Community
College
11000 Pleasant Valley Blvd.
Parma, OH 44130

School of Radiography
Shawnee State University
940 Second St.
Portsmouth, OH 45662

School of Radiography
Kent State University/
Salem Campus
2491 SR 45 South
Salem, OH 44460

School of Radiography
Providence Hospital, Inc.
1912 Hayes Ave.
Sandusky, OH 44870

School of Radiography
Community Hospital of
Springfield and Clark Cty
2615 E. High St.
Springfield, OH 45501

School of Radiography
Jefferson Community
　College
4000 Sunset Blvd.
Steubenville, OH 43952

School of Radiography
Mercy College of NW Ohio
2221 Madison Ave.
Toledo, OH
　43624-1132

School of Radiography
Owens Community
　College
P.O. Box 10,000
Toledo, OH 43699

School of Radiography
St. Elizabeth Health Center
Belmont and Park Ave.
Youngstown, OH 44501

School of Radiography
West Residential Care System-
　NOSD Medical Center
500 Gypsy Ln.
Youngstown, OH 44501

School of Radiography
Muskingum Area Technical
　College
1555 Newark Rd.
Zanesville, OH 43701

Oklahoma

School of Radiography
Western Oklahoma State
　College
2801 N. Main
Altus, OK 73521-1397

School of Radiography
Autry Technology Center
1201 W. Willow
Enid, OK 73703

School of Radiography
Great Plains Area Vocational/
　Technical School
4500 W. Lee Blvd.
Lawton, OK 73505

School of Radiography
Rose State College
6420 SE Fifteenth St.
Midwest City, OK
　73110-2799

School of Radiologic Technology
Bacone College
2299 Old Bacone Rd.
Muskogee, OK 74403

School of Radiography
Metro Area Vo-Tech School
1720 Springlake Dr.
Oklahoma City, OK 73111

School of Radiography
U of Oklahoma College
　of Allied Health
Box 26901, CHB 450
Oklahoma City, OK 73190

School of Radiography
SW Oklahoma State University
409 E. Mississippi
Sayre, OK 73662

School of Radiography
Meridian Technology Center
1312 S. Sangre Rd.
Stillwater, OK 74074

School of Radiography
 Tulsa Cty Area Vo-Tech
 School
 3420 S. Memorial Dr.
 Tulsa, OK 74145-1309

School of Radiography
 Tulsa Community College
 6111 E. Skelly Dr., Room 200
 Tulsa, OK 74135

Oregon

School of Radiography
 Oregon Institute of Technology
 3201 Campus Dr./Dept. Med.
  Imaging
 Klamath Falls, OR 97601

School of Radiography
 Portland Community College
 12000 SW Forty-ninth Ave.
 P.O. Box 19000
 Portland, OR 97280-0990

Pennsylvania

School of Radiography
 Northampton Community
  College
 3835 Green Pond Rd.
 Bethlehem, PA 18020

School of Radiography
 Bradford Regional
  Medical Center
 116 Interstate Pkwy.
 Bradford, PA 16701

School of Radiography
 Holy Spirit Hospital
 503 N. Twenty-first St.
 Camp Hill, PA 17011-2288

School of Radiography
 Clearfield Hospital
 809 Turnpike Ave.,
 P.O. Box 992
 Clearfield, PA 16830

School of Radiography
 Brandywine Hospital
 201 Reeceville Rd.
 Coatesville, PA 19320-1536

School of Radiography
 Mount Aloysius College
 7373 Admiral Peary Hwy.
 Cresson, PA 16630

School of Radiography
 College Misericordia
 301 Lake St.
 Dallas, PA 18612

School of Radiography
 Allegheny University
  Hospitals
 60 E. Township Line Rd.
 Elkins Park, PA 19027

School of Radiography
 Gannon University
 109 University Sq.
 Erie, PA 16541-0001

School of Radiography
 Northwest Medical Center-
  Franklin Campus
 1 Spruce St.
 Franklin, PA 16323

School of Radiography
 Pinnacle Health
  at Polycl. Hosp.
 2601 N. Third St.
 Harrisburg, PA 17110

School of Radiography
Hazelton-St. Joseph
Medical Center
687 N. Church St.
Hazleton, PA 18201

School of Radiography
Monsour Medical Center
70 Lincoln Way E
Jeannette, PA 15644

School of Radiography
Conemaugh Valley Memorial
Hospital
1086 Franklin St.
Johnstown, PA 15905

School of Radiography
Lee Hospital
320 Main St.
Johnstown, PA 15901

School of Radiography
Armstrong County Memorial
Hospital
One Nolte Dr.
Kittanning, PA 16201

School of Radiography
Lancaster Institute for Health
Education
143 E. Lemon St.
Lancaster, PA 17602

School of Radiography
Mansfield University
Elliott Hall
Mansfield, PA 16933

School of Radiography
RMC-Ohio Valley General
Hospital
25 Heckel Rd.
McKees Rocks, PA 15136

School of Radiography
Community College
of Allegheny County
595 Beatty Rd.
Monroeville, PA 15146

School of Radiography
Allegheny Valley Hospital
1300 Carlisle St.
Natrona Heights, PA 15065

School of Radiography
St. Francis Hospital
1000 Mercer St.
New Castle, PA 16101

School of Radiologic Technology
Penn State University/New
Kensington
3550 Seventh St. Rd.
New Kensington, PA
15068-1798

School of Radiography
Albert Einstein Medical Center
5501 Old York Rd.
Philadelphia, PA 19141

School of Radiography
Allegheny University
of Health Science
Broad and Vine Streets
Philadelphia, PA 19102

School of Radiography
Community College
of Philadelphia
1700 Spring Garden St.
Philadelphia, PA 19130

School of Radiography
Holy Family College
Grant & Frankford Avenues
Philadelphia, PA 19114

School of Radiography
  Temple University Hospital
  3401 N. Broad St.
  Philadelphia, PA 19140

School of Radiography
  Thomas Jefferson University
  130 S. Ninth St., Room 1004
  Philadelphia, PA 19107

School of Radiography
  RMC-Allegheny General
    Hospital
  320 E. North Ave.
  Pittsburgh, PA 15212

School of Radiography
  UPMC Health System
  200 Lothrop St.
  Pittsburgh, PA
    15213-2582

School of Radiography
  Western School of Health and
    Business Career
  421 Seventh Ave.
  Pittsburgh, PA 15219-1907

School of Radiography
  Reading Hospital
    and Medical Center
  P.O. Box 16052
  Reading, PA 19612-6052

School of Radiography
  St. Joseph's Hospital
  12th and Walnut St.,
    Box 316
  Reading, PA 19603

School of Radiography
  Pennsylvania State University
  200 University Dr.
  Schuylkill Haven, PA 17972

School of Radiography
  Community Medical Center
  1822 Mulberry St.
  Scranton, PA 18510

School of Radiography
  Sewickley Valley Hospital
  720 Blackburn Rd.
  Sewickley, PA 15143

School of Radiography
  Sharon Regional Health
    System
  740 E. State St.
  Sharon, PA 16146

School of Radiography
  Crozer-Chester Medical Center
  One Medical Center Blvd.
  Upland, PA 19013-2571

School of Radiography
  Washington Hospital
  155 Wilson
  Washington, PA 15301

School of Radiography
  Wilkes-Barre General
    Hospital
  North River & Auburn Streets
  Wilkes-Barre, PA 18764

School of Radiography
  Pennsylvania College
    of Technology
  1 College Ave./ Dif21
  Williamsport, PA 17701

School of Radiography
  Abington Memorial Hospital
  2500 Maryland Rd.
  Willow Grove, PA 19090

Puerto Rico

School of Radiography
Universidad Central Del Caribe
Call Box 60-327
Bayamon, PR 00960

School of Radiography
University of Puerto Rico
Med Sci Campus,
P.O. Box 365067
San Juan, PR 00936-5067

Rhode Island

School of Radiography
Community College
of Rhode Island
1762 Louisquisset Pike
Lincoln, RI 02865

School of Radiography
Rhode Island Hospital
593 Eddy St./SW Pavilion
Providence, RI 02902

South Carolina

School of Radiography
Anderson Area Medical Center
800 N. Fant St.
Anderson, SC 29621

School of Radiography
Trident Technical College
7000 Rivers Ave.,
P.O. Box 118067
Charleston, SC 29423-8067

School of Radiography
Midlands Technical College
P.O. Box 2408
Columbia, SC 29202

School of Radiography
Horry-Georgetown Technical
College
2050 Hwy. 501 East
P.O. Box 1966
Conway, SC 29528-6066

School of Radiography
Florence-Darlington Technical
College
P.O. Drawer 100548
Florence, SC 29501-0548

School of Radiography
Greenville Technical College
P.O. Box 5616
Greenville, SC
29606-5616

School of Radiography
Piedmont Technical College
Emerald Rd.,
P.O. Drawer 1467
Greenwood, SC 29646-1467

School of Radiography
Orangeburg-Calhoun Technical
College
3250 St. Matthews Rd. NE
Orangeburg, SC 29118

School of Radiography
York Technical College
452 S. Anderson Rd.
Rock Hill, SC 29730

School of Radiography
Spartanburg Technical
College
P.O. Box 4386
Spartanburg, SC 29303-4386

South Dakota

School of Radiography
Avera St. Lukes
305 S. State St.,
  Box 4450
Aberdeen, SD 57401

School of Radiography
Rapid City Regional
  Hospital
353 Fairmont Blvd.
Rapid City, SD 57701

School of Radiography
McKennan Hospital
800 E. Twenty-first St.
Sioux Falls, SD 57101

School of Radiography
Sioux Valley Hospital
1100 S. Euclid Ave.,
  P.O. Box 5039
Sioux Falls, SD 57105

School of Radiography
Sacred Heart Hospital
501 Summit
Yankton, SD 57078

Tennessee

School of Radiography
Chattanooga State Technical
  Community College
4501 Amnicola Hwy.
Chattanooga, TN 37406

School of Radiography
Columbia State Community
  College
P.O. Box 1315
Columbia, TN 38402-1315

School of Radiography
Etsu-Paramedical Center
1000 W. "E" St.
Elizabethton, TN 37643

School of Radiography
Volunteer State Community
  College
1480 Nashville Pike
Gallatin, TN 37066

School of Radiography, Oak
  Ridge Campus
Roane State Community
  College
Patton Ln.
Harriman, TN 37748

School of Radiography
Jackson State Community
  College
2046 N. Parkway St.
Jackson, TN 38301

School of Radiography
University of Tennessee
  Medical Center
  at Knoxville
Knoxville Unit 1924
  Alcoa Hwy.
Knoxville, TN 37920

School of Radiography
Baptist Memorial College
  of Health Sciences
1003 Monroe
Memphis, TN 38104

School of Radiography
Methodist Healthcare
1265 Union Ave.
Memphis, TN 38104

School of Radiography
St. Joseph Hospital
220 Overton Ave.,
P.O. Box 178
Memphis, TN 38101

School of Radiography
Shelby State Community
College
P.O. Box 40568
Memphis, TN
38174-0568

School of Radiography
Nashville Metro General
Hospital
72 Hermitage Ave.
Nashville, TN 37210

Texas

School of Radiography
Hendrick Medical Center
1242 North Nineteenth
Abilene, TX 79601

School of Radiography
Amarillo College
P.O. Box 447
Amarillo, TX 79178

School of Radiography
(Riverside Camp)
Austin Community College
1020 Grove Blvd.
Austin, TX 78741

School of Radiography
Baptist Hospital
of SE Texas
P.O. Drawer 1591
Beaumont, TX 77704

School of Radiography
Lamar University
P.O. Box 10061
Beaumont, TX 77710

School of Radiography
Scenic Mountain
Medical Center
1601 W. Eleventh Pl.
Big Spring, TX 79720

School of Radiography
University of Texas-
Brownsville and Texas
Southern College
80 Ft. Brown
Brownsville, TX 78520-4993

School of Radiography
Blinn College
301 Post Office St.
Bryan, TX 77801

School of Radiography
Delmar College
101 Baldwin
Corpus Christi, TX 78404

School of Radiologic Technology
Baylor University
Medical Center
3500 Gaston Ave.
Dallas, TX 75246

School of Radiography
El Centro College
Main & Lamar Streets
Dallas, TX 75202-3604

School of Radiography
El Paso Community College
P.O. Box 20500
El Paso, TX 79998

Radiology Specialist Course/
US Army
Academy of Health Science/
A MEDDC & S
MCCS-HCR/3151 Scott Rd.
Ft. Sam Houston, TX 78234

School of Radiography
JPS Institute of Health Career
Development
2400 Circle Dr., Suite 100
Fort Worth, TX 76119

School of Radiography
Galveston College
4015 Ave. "Q"
Galveston, TX
77550-2782

School of Medical Radiography
Harris County Hospital Dis/
B Taub Gen
1504 Taub Loop
Houston, TX 77030

School of Radiography
Houston Community College
System
5514 Clara
Houston, TX 77041

School of Radiography
Memorial Hospital System
7600 Beechnut
Houston, TX 77074

School of Radiography
Tarrant County Jr
College-N E
828 Harwood Rd.
Hurst, TX
76054-3299

School of Radiography
Kilgore College
1100 Broadway
Kilgore, TX 75662

School of Radiography
Laredo Community
College
W. End Washington St.
Laredo, TX 78040

School of Radiography
Covenent Medical Center
3801 Nineteenth St.,
Suite 500
Lubbock, TX 79410

School of Radiography
South Plains College-
Lubbock
1302 Main
Lubbock, TX 79401

School of Radiography
Angelina College
P.O. Box 1768
Lufkin, TX 75901

School of Radiography
South Texas Community
College
3201 W. Pecan Blvd.
McAllen, TX 78501

School of Radiography
Midland College
3600 N. Garfield
Midland, TX 79705

School of Radiography
Odessa College
201 W. University Blvd.
Odessa, TX 79764

School of Radiography
San Jacinto College Central
8060 Spencer Hwy.
P.O. Box 2007
Pasadena, TX 77505

School of Radiography
Baptist Memorial Hospital
111 Dallas St. "3F"
San Antonio, TX 78205

School of Radiography
St. Philip's College
1801 Martin Luther King Dr.
San Antonio, TX 78203-2098

School of Radiography
School of Health Care Science/
USAF
381 TRS/XWBF 917
Missile Rd.
Sheppard AFB, TX 76311-2246

School of Radiography
Wadley Regional
Medical Center
1000 Pine St.
Texarkana, TX 75501

School of Radiography
Tyler Junior College
P.O. Box 9020
Tyler, TX 75711

School of Radiography
Citizens Medical Center
2701 Hospital Dr.
Victoria, TX 77901

School of Radiography
McLennan Community College
1400 College Dr.
Waco, TX 76708

School of Radiography
Wharton County Junior College
911 Boling Hwy.
Wharton, TX 77488

School of Radiography
Midwestern State University
3410 Taft Blvd.
Wichita Falls, TX 76308

Utah

College of Health Professions-
Radiography
Weber State University
3925 University Circle
Ogden, UT 84408-3925

School of Radiography
Utah Valley Regional
Medical Center
1034 N. 500 West
Provo, UT 84603

School of Radiography
Salt Lake Community College
4600 S. Redwood Rd.,
P.O. Box 30808
Salt Lake City, UT 84130

Vermont

School of Radiography
Champlain College
163 S. Willard St.
P.O. Box 670
Burlington, VT 05402

School of Radiography
Rutland Regional
Medical Center
160 Allen St.
Rutland, VT 05701

Virginia

School of Radiography
Northern Virginia Community
College
8333 Little River Turnpike
Annandale, VA 22003

School of Radiography
University of Virginia Health
Sciences Center
Rad 170 Jefferson Park Ave.
Charlottesville, VA 22908

School of Radiography
Mary Washington Hospital
1001 Sam Perry Blvd.
Fredericksburg, VA 22401

School of Radiography
Rockingham Memorial
Hospital
235 Cantrell Ave.
Harrisonburg, VA 22801-3293

School of Radiography
Central Virginia Community
College
3506 Wards Rd.
Lynchburg, VA 24502

School of Radiography
Rvrsd Sch Hlth Occ
& Nwprt P S
12420 Warwick Blvd.,
Suite 6-G
Newport News, VA 23606

School of Radiography
Southside Regional
Medical Center
801 S. Adams St.
Petersburg, VA 23803

Naval Radiologic Technology
Program
Naval School of Health
Science
1001 Holcomb Rd.
Portsmouth, VA 23708

School of Radiography
Southwest Virginia
Community College
Box SVCC
Richlands, VA 24641

School of Radiography
St Mary's Hospital
5801 Bremo Rd.
Richmond, VA 23226

School of Radiography/Dept. of
Radiography Science
Virginia Commonwealth
University/Medical College
Box 980495
Richmond, VA 23298-0495

School of Radiography
Roanoke Memorial
Hospitals
P.O. Box 13367
Roanoke, VA 24033-3367

School of Radiography
Virginia Western Community
College
P.O. Box 14007
Roanoke, VA 24038

School of Radiologic Technology
Tidewater Community College
1700 College Crescent
Virginia Beach, VA 23456

128   *Opportunities in Medical Imaging Careers*

School of Radiologic Technology
Winchester Medical Center
1840 Amherst St.,
P.O. Box 3340
Winchester, VA 22601

Washington

School of Radiography
Bellevue Community College
B-243 3000 Landerholm
Circle SE
Bellevue, WA 98007-6484

School of Radiography
Pima Medical Institute
1627 Eastlake Ave. East
Seattle, WA 98102

School of Radiography
Holy Family Hospital
N. 5633 Lidgerwood
Spokane, WA 99207

School of Radiography
Tacoma Community
College
6501 S. Nineteenth St.
Tacoma, WA 98466

School of Radiography
Wenatchee Valley College
1300 Fifth St.
Wenatchee, WA 98801

School of Radiography
Yakima Valley Comm
College
P.O. Box 1647
Yakima, WA 98907

West Virginia

School of Radiography
Bluefield State College
219 Rock St.
Bluefield, WV 24701

School of Radiography
University of Charleston
2300 MacCorkle Ave. SE
Charleston, WV 25304

School of Radiography
United Hospital Center, Inc.
P.O. Box 1680/#3,
Hospital Plaza
Clarksburg, WV 26302-1680

School of Radiography
St. Mary's Hospital
2900 First Ave.
Huntington, WV 25702

School of Radiography
West Virginia University
Hospitals
Medical Center Dr.
P.O. Box 8062
Morgantown, WV 26505-8136

School of Radiography
Southern West Virginia
Community and Technical
College
P.O. Box 2900, Dempsey
Branch Rd.
Mt. Gay, WV 25637

School of Radiography
Camden-Clark Memorial
Hospital
P.O. Box 718
Parkersburg, WV 26102

School of Radiography
Ohio Valley Medical
Center Inc.
2000 Eoff St.
Wheeling, WV 26003

School of Radiologic Technology
Wheeling Hospital
1 Medical Park
Wheeling, WV 26003

Wisconsin

School of Radiography
Lakeshore Technical College
1290 North Ave.
Cleveland, WI 53015-1414

School of Radiography
Chippewa Valley Technical
College
620 W. Clairemont Ave.
Eau Claire, WI 54701

School of Radiography
Bellin Memorial Hospital
744 S. Webster Ave.,
P.O. Box 23400
Green Bay, WI 54305

School of Radiography
Blackhawk Technical College
6004 Prairie Rd.
P.O. Box 5009
Janesville, WI 53547

School of Radiography
Western Wisconsin Technical
College
304 N. Sixth St.
P.O. Box 908
La Crosse, WI 54601-0908

School of Radiography
Madison Area Technical
College
3550 Anderson St.
Madison, WI 53704

School of Radiography
University of Wisconsin
Hospital & Clinic
600 Highland Ave.
Madison, WI
53792-3252

School of Radiography
St. Joseph's Hospital
611 St. Joseph Ave.
Marshfield, WI 54449

School of Radiography
Columbia/St. Marys
Hospital
2323 N. Lake Dr.,
P.O. Box 503
Milwaukee, WI 53211

School of Radiography
Froedtert Memorial Lutheran
Hospital
9200 W. Wisconsin Ave.
Milwaukee, WI 53226

School of Radiography
Milwaukee Area Technical
College
700 W. State St.
Milwaukee, WI 53233

School of Radiography
St. Luke's Medical Center
2900 W. Oklahoma Ave.
Milwaukee, WI 53215-2901

School of Radiography
St. Michael's Hospital
2400 W. Villard Ave.
Milwaukee, WI 53209

School of Radiography
Theda Clark Regional Medical
Center
130 Second St., P.O. Box 2021
Neenah, WI 54957

School of Radiography
Affinity Health System
631 Hazel St., P.O. Box 1100
Oshkosh, WI 54902-1100

School of Radiologic Technology
All Saints Healthcare System
Inc.
1320 Wisconsin Ave.
Racine, WI 53403

School of Radiography
Northcentral Technical College
1000 Campus Dr.
Wausau, WI 54401

Wyoming

School of Radiography
Casper College
125 College Dr.
Casper, WY 82601

School of Radiography
Laramie County Community
College
1400 E. College Dr.
Cheyenne, WY 82007

APPENDIX E

ACCREDITED DIAGNOSTIC MEDICAL SONOGRAPHER PROGRAMS

Alabama

Wallace State College
DMS Program
P.O. Box 2000
Hanceville, AL 35077-2000

Arizona

Pima Medical Institute
3350 E. Grant Rd.
Tucson, AZ 85716

Arkansas

University of Arkansas for
Medical Sciences
4301 W. Markham St.
Mail Slot #563
Little Rock, AR 72205

California

Loma Linda University
School of Allied Health
Professionals
Diagnostic Medical
Sonographer Program
Loma Linda, CA 92350

Orange Coast College
2701 Fairview Rd.
Costa Mesa, CA 92628

Colorado

Centura Health/The Penrose/St.
Francis Healthcare System
Diagnostic Medical
Sonography Program
2215 N. Cascade Ave.
Colorado Springs, CO 80933

University Hospital/University of
Colorado Health Science
Center
Department of Ultrasound,
Box C-277
4200 E. Ninth Ave.
Denver, CO 80262

Delaware

Delaware Technical and
Community College
333 Shipley St.
Wilmington, DE 19801

131

District of Columbia

George Washington University
2300 K St. NW
Washington, DC 20037

Florida

Broward Community College
Diagnostic Medical
Sonography Program
1000 Coconut Creek Blvd.
Coconut Creek, FL 33066

Florida Hospital College
of Health Sciences
800 Lake Estelle Dr.
Orlando, FL 32803

Hillsborough Community College
Diagnostic Medical
Sonographer Program
P.O. Box 30030
Tampa, FL 33630-3030

Miami Dade Community College
Medical Center Campus
Jackson Memorial Hospital
Consortium
950 NW Twentieth St.
Miami, FL 33127-4693

Valencia Community College
P.O. Box 3028
Orlando, FL 32806

Georgia

Grady Health System
Box 26095
80 Butler St. SE
Atlanta, GA 30335

Medical College of Georgia
Diagnostic Medical
Sonographer Program
AE-1003
Augusta, GA
30912-0600

Illinois

South Suburban College
15800 S. State St.
South Holland, IL 60473

Triton College
Diagnostic Medical
Sonographer Program
2000 N. Fifth Ave.
River Grove, IL 60171

Iowa

Mercy College of Health Sciences
928 Sixth Ave.
Des Moines, IA 50309-1239

University of Iowa Hospitals
and Clinic
Diagnostic Medical
Sonographer Program
Radiology Dept./C726 G4
Iowa City, IA 50309

Kentucky

University of Louisville
School of Allied Health
Sciences
Abell Administration
Center
Louisville, KY 40292

West Kentucky State Vocational
   Technical
   Diagnostic Medical
   Sonographer Program
   Blandville Rd.
   P.O. Box 7408
   Paducah, KY 42002-7408

Maryland

Johns Hopkins Hospital
   600 N. Wolfe St.
   Radiology Administration
   B-179
   Baltimore, MD 21287

Montgomery College
   7600 Takoma Ave.
   Takoma Park, MD 20912

UMBC Continuing Education
   UMBC Technology Center
   1450 S. Rolling Rd.
   Cantonsville, MD 21228

Massachusetts

Bunker Hill Community College
   250 New Rutherford Ave.
   Boston, MA 02129-2991

Middlesex Community College
   Diagnostic Medical
   Sonographer Program
   Springs Rd.
   Bedford, MA 01730

Springfield Technical
   Community College
   One Armory Sq.
   Springfield, MA 01105

Michigan

Henry Ford Hospital
   Diagnostic Medical
   Sonographer Program
   2799 W. Grand Blvd.
   Detroit, MI 48202

Jackson Community
   College
   Diagnostic Medical
   Sonographer Program
   2111 Emmons Rd.
   Jackson, MI 49201

Oakland Community
   College
   Diagnostic Medical
   Sonographer Program
   22322 Rutland Dr.
   Southfield, MI 48075

Providence Hospital
   16001 W. Nine Mile Rd.
   Southfield, MI 48037

Minnesota

The College of St. Catherine's
   601 Twenty-fifth Ave., South
   Minneapolis, MN 55454

Mayo Foundation
   Diagnostic Medical
   Sonographer Program
   200 First St. S.W.
   Rochester, MN 55905

Missouri

St. Louis Community College
   at Forest Park
   Diagnostic Medical
   Sonography Program
   5600 Oakland Ave.
   St. Louis, MO 63110

Nebraska

Nebraska Methodist College
   of Nursing and Allied
   Health
   8501 W. Dodge Rd.
   Omaha, NE 68114

University of Nebraska Medical
   Center
   600 S. Forty-second St.
   Omaha, NE 68198

New Jersey

Bergen County Community
   College
   Diagnostic Medical
   Sonography Program
   400 Paramus Rd.
   Paramus, NJ 07652-1595

Gloucester County College
   1400 Tanyard Rd.
   Sewell, NJ 08080

University of Medicine and
   Dentistry of New Jersey
   School of Health Related
   Professions
   Diagnostic Medical
   Sonography Program
   65 Bergen St.
   Newark, NJ 07107-3006

New York

Hudson Valley Community
   College
   80 Vandenburgh Ave.
   Troy, NY 12180

New York University
   11 W. Forty-second St.,
   Room 518
   New York, NY 10013-8083

Rochester Institute of Technology
   Diagnostic Medical
   Sonographer Program
   One Lomb Memorial Dr.
   P.O. Box 9887
   Rochester, NY 14623-0887

SUNY Health Science Center—
   Brooklyn College of Health
   Related Professions
   Diagnostic Medical
   Sonographer Program
   450 Clarkson Ave.
   Box 11203
   Brooklyn, NY 11203

Western Suffolk BOCES
   Northport VA Medical Center
   79 Middleville Rd.
   Building 62
   Northport, NY 11768

North Carolina

Caldwell Community College
   and Technical Institute
   Diagnostic Medical
   Sonographer Program
   1000 Hickory Blvd.
   Hudson, NC 28638

Forsyth Technical Community
  College
2100 Silas Creek Pkwy.
Winston-Salem, NC 27103

Pitt Community College
  Diagnostic Medical
  Sonography Program
P.O. Drawer 7007
Greenville, NC 27835-7007

Ohio

Central Ohio Technical
  College
  Diagnostic Medical
  Sonographer Program
1179 University Dr.
Newark, OH 43055

Kettering College
  of Medical Arts
  Diagnostic Medical
  Sonographer Program
3737 Southern Blvd.
Kettering, OH 45429

Lorain County Community
  College
1005 N. Abbe Rd.
Elyria, OH 44035

Michael J. Owens Technical
  College
  Diagnostic Medical
  Sonographer Program
P.O. Box 10,000—Oregon Rd.
Toledo, OH 43699-1947

Oklahoma

University of Oklahoma
  at Oklahoma City
  Diagnostic Medical
  Sonographer Program
Box 26901
Oklahoma City, OK 73190

Pennsylvania

Community College of
  Allegheny County—Boyce
  Campus
  Diagnostic Medical
  Sonographer Program
595 Beatty Rd.
Monroeville, PA 15146

Lancaster Institute for Health
  Education
143 E. Lemon St.
Lancaster, PA 17602

Polyclinic Medical Center
  Diagnostic Medical
  Sonographer Program
2601 N. Third St.
Harrisburg, PA 17110

Thomas Jefferson University
  Diagnostic Medical
  Sonographer Program
130 S. Ninth St., Room 1004
Philadelphia, PA 19107

Western School of Health and
  Business Careers
421 Seventh Ave.
Pittsburgh, PA 15219-1907

Rhode Island

Rhode Island Hospital
593 Eddy St.
Providence, RI 02902

Tennessee

Baptist Memorial College
    of Health Sciences
1003 Monroe Ave., 3rd Floor
Memphis, TN 38104

Chattanooga State Technical
    Community College
535 Chestnut St., Suite 112
Chattanooga, TN 37406

Texas

Austin Community
    College
Diagnostic Medical
    Sonographer Program
1020 Grove Blvd.
Austin, TX 78714

Del Mar College
Diagnostic Medical
    Sonographer Program
101 Baldwin and Ayers Streets
Corpus Christi, TX 78404

El Centro College
Diagnostic Medical
    Sonographer Program
Main & Lamar
Dallas, TX 75202

El Paso Community College
Diagnostic Medical
    Sonographer Program
P.O. Box 20500
El Paso, TX 79998

Tyler Junior College
P.O. Box 9020
Tyler, TX 75711

Virginia

Southwest Virginia Community
    College
P.O. Box SVCC
Richlands, VA 24641-1510

Tidewater Community College
1700 College Crescent
Virginia Beach, VA 23456

Washington

Bellevue Community College
Diagnostic Medical
    Sonographer Program
3000 Landerholm Circle
P.O. Box 92700
Room B243
Bellevue, WA 98009-2037

Seattle University
Diagnostic Medical
    Sonographer Program
900 Broadway and Madison
Seattle, WA 98122

West Virginia

The College of West Virginia
609 S. Kanawha St.
P.O. Box AG
Beckley, WV 25802-0789

West Virginia University Hospital
Diagnostic Medical
Sonographer Program
P.O. Box 8062
Morgantown, WV 26506

Wisconsin

Chippewa Valley Technical
College
Diagnostic Medical
Sonographer Program
620 W. Clairemont Ave.
Eau Claire, WI 54701

Columbia St. Mary's Hospital
2323 N. Luke Dr.
P.O. Box 503
Milwaukee, WI 53211

St. Francis Hospital
Diagnostic Medical
Sonographer Program
3237 S. Sixteenth St.
Milwaukee, WI 53215

St. Luke's Medical Center
Diagnostic Medical
Sonographer Program
2900 W. Oklahoma Ave.
Milwaukee, WI 53215

University of Wisconsin Hospital
and Clinics
Department of Radiology
Diagnostic Medical
Sonography Program
600 Highland Ave.
Madison, WI 53792

STATES THAT REQUIRE LICENSURE FOR PRACTICE OF RADIOLOGIC TECHNOLOGY

Arizona

State of Arizona
  Medical Radiological
  Technology
  Board of Examiners
  4814 S. Fortieth St.
  Phoenix, AZ 85040

California

State of California
  Radiological Health Branch
  714 P St.
  Sacramento, CA 95814

Colorado

Colorado State Medical Board
  1560 Broadway, Suite 1300
  Denver, CO 80202

Connecticut

Department of Public Health
  Bureaus of Health Systems
  Registration
  Calitol Ave.
  MS#12APP
  Box 340308
  Hartford, CT 06134

Delaware

State of Delaware Office
  of Radiation Control
  Robbins Building
  P.O. Box 637
  Dover, DE 19903

Florida

State of Florida HRS Radiation
  Control
  1317 Winewood Blvd.
  Tallahassee, FL 32301

Hawaii

State of Hawaii Radiologic
    Technology Board
    Departments of Health Noise
    and Radiation Branch
    591 Ala Moana Blvd.
    Honolulu, HI 96813-2498

Illinois

State of Illinois Division of
    Radiologic Technologist
    Certification
    Illinois Department of Nuclear
    Safety
    P.O. Box 1964
    1035 Outer Park Dr.
    Springfield, IL 62704

Indiana

Radiological Health Division
    Director
    Indiana State Board of Health
    P.O. Box 1964
    Indianapolis, IN 46206

Iowa

Bureau of Environmental Health
    State of Iowa
    Department of Health
    Lucas State Office Building
    Des Moines, IA 50319-0075

Kentucky

Radiation & Product Safety
    Branch
    275 E. Main St.
    Frankfort, KY 40621

Louisiana

Louisiana State Radiologic
    Technology
    Board of Examiners
    3108 Cleary Ave., Suite 207
    Metairie, LA 70002

Maine

Radiologic Technology
    Board of Examiners
    State House Station #35
    Augusta, ME 04333

Maryland

State of Maryland Public Health
    Engineer
    2500 Broening Hwy.
    Baltimore, MD 21224

Massachusetts

Radiation Control Program
    Department of Public Health
    150 Tremont St., 11th Floor
    Boston, MA 02111

Minnesota

Department of Health-Radiation
    Control Section
    121 E. Seventh Pl.
    P.O. Box 64675
    St. Paul, MN 55164

Missouri

State Board of Health
    Professional Licensure
    P.O. Box 1700
    Jackson, MS 39215

Montana

Board of Radiologic Technology
   1424 Ninth Ave.
   Helena, MT 59620

Nebraska

Department of Health
   Division of Radiologic Health
   301 Centennial Mall South
   Lincoln, NE 68509-5007

New Jersey

Bureau of Radiologic Health
   CN415
   Trenton, NJ 08625

New Mexico

State of New Mexico Radiation
   Protection Bureau
   P.O. Box 968
   Sante Fe, NM 87504

New York

New York State Dept. of Health
   Bureau of Environmental
   Radiation Protection
   2 University Pl., Room 325
   Albany, NY 12203-3313

Ohio

Ohio Department of Health
   Radiologic Technology Section
   246 N. High St.
   P.O. Box 118
   Columbus, OH 43266

Oregon

Health Licensing Boards
   Oregon State Health Division
   P.O. Box 231
   Portland, OR 97207

Pennsylvania

Bureau of Professional and
   Occupational Affairs
   State Board of Medicine
   P.O. Box 2649
   Harrisburg, PA 17105-2649

Rhode Island

Rhode Island Department
   of Health
   Division of Professional
   Registration
   3 Capitol Hill
   Providence, RI 02908

Tennessee

Tennessee Board of Medical
   Examiners
   283 Plus Park Blvd.
   Nashville, TN 37247-1010

Texas

Texas Department of Health
   Medical Technology Program
   1100 W. Forty-ninth St.
   Austin, TX 78756-3199

Utah

Bureau of Health Professions
  Licensing
Division of Occupational and
  Professional Licensing
160 E. 300 South
Salt Lake City, UT 84145-0805

Vermont

Board of Radiologic Technology
Office of the Secretary of State
Pavillion Office Building
Montpelier, VT 05609

Virginia

Department of Health Professions
6606 W. Broad St., 4th Floor
Richmond, VI 23230

Washington

Washington State Office of
  Radiation
Olympic Building S. 220
217 Pine St.
Seattle, WA 98101

West Virginia

West Virginia Radiologic
  Technology
Board of Examiners
1715 Flat Top Rd.
Cool Ridge, WV 25825

Wyoming

The State of Wyoming
Board of Radiologic
  Technologists Examiners
1312 Monroe Ave.
Cheyenne, WY 82001

GLOSSARY

Aliasing: Interference caused by beats or signals between the emitted and received signals of a Doppler ultrasound system.

Alpha particle: A group of four particles (two protons and two neutrons) emitted from an unstable nucleus.

Alpha ray: A stream of alpha particles emitted from a large group of unstable nuclei.

Annular array: A group of transducers, antennas, or other detectors arranged in an annulus (ring).

Attenuation: The decrease in dose rate of radiation passing through a material.

Background radiation: In a given area, the sum total of radioactivity from cosmic rays, natural radioactive materials, and whatever may have been introduced into the area.

Becquerd (Bg):   A unit of radioactive material. Thirty-seven billion curies equal one becquerd.

Charge: An ionized particle. If an electron is removed from an atom, two charges are formed. The displaced electron is the negative charge, and the rest of the atom is the positive charge.

Sometimes the electron becomes attached to an otherwise neutral atom, thus giving the atom a negative charge.

Coil: Single or multiple loops of wire (or other electrical conductor, such as tubing) designed either to produce a magnetic field from current flowing through the wire, or to detect a changing magnetic field by voltage induced in the wire.

Continuous wave (CW) NMR: A technique for studying nuclear magnetic resonance (NMR) by continuously inputting radio-frequency radiation to the sample and applying either the total range of radiation frequencies or the magnetic field through the total range of resonance values; this technique has been largely superseded by pulse NMR techniques.

Contrast: The relative difference of the signal intensities in two adjacent regions.

Curie (Ci):   A unit of radioactive material.

Decay: The transformation of one element into another by the emission of alpha or beta particles from the nucleus.

Diamagnetic material: A substance that is repelled by magnetism.

Dielectric: Material that insulates two conductors of electricity from each other.

Dielectric constant: A number indicating the efficiency of a dielectric as an insulator. The higher the number, the greater the efficiency.

Direct ionization: Ionization brought about by the direct action of the ionizing cause.

Eddy current: An induced electric current circulating through the entire body of a mass. Such currents are converted into heat, causing serious waste.

Electromagnet: A magnet created by passing an electric current through a coil of wire. A core of magnetic material is placed in the center of the coil to concentrate the magnetic field.

Electromagnetic spectrum: The range of energies of electromagnetic radiations.

Electromagnetic wave: A wave produced by the oscillation of an electric charge.

Electron volt (eV):   An energy unit; the amount of energy acquired when an electron falls through a potential difference of one volt.

emf: Elecromotive force. Other names are *potential difference* and *voltage.*

Endoscopic: Refers to the examination of a body cavity by means of an instrument.

Ferromagnetic material: Material that makes a good magnet.

Field: An area of influence.

Fourier transform: A mathematical procedure to separate the frequency components of a signal from its amplitudes as a function of time. The Fourier transform is used to generate the spectrum from the FID in pulse nuclear magnetic resonance techniques and is essential to most imaging techniques.

Frequency (FT):   The number of vibrations or cycles in a unit of time. For elecromagnetic radiation, such as radio waves, the old unit cycles per second (cps) has been replaced by the SI unit hertz (Hz).

Gamma ray: When an unstable nucleus has emitted an alpha or beta particle, it is often left with excess energy. This is given out as a gamma ray. It is usually associated with beta emission rather than alpha emission.

Gauss (G):   A unit of magnetic flux density in the metric system. The earth's magnetic field is approximately 0.5 gauss, depending on location. The currently preferred (SI) unit is the tesla. One tesla equals ten thousand gauss.

Gradient magnetic field: A magnetic field that changes in strength along a certain given direction.

Ground: The earth (or ground) is regarded as a huge reservoir of electrons. Any charged body connected to ground will become neutralized.

Half-life: The time taken for the radioactivity of a radioisotope to decay to half its original value.

Hertz: A measurement of frequency. One hertz equals one cycle per second.

Hysteresis: A lagging or retardation of the effect, such as when the magnetization of a piece of iron or steel, caused by a magnetic field that varies through a cycle of values, lags behind the field.

Indirect ionization: Ionization caused secondarily to the action of the original ionizing influence, not by the original ionizing influence itself.

Insulator: A substance that tends to oppose the passage of electric current.

Inverse square law: The intensity of radiation at any point is inversely proportional to the square of the distance of that point from the source of radiation.

Ionization: Ionization occurs when an electron is removed from the orbit of a neutral atom and the atom is left with an overall positive charge. The positively charged atom is called a positive ion, and the electron is called a negative ion.

Ionizing radiation: Any form of radiation that causes ionization; for example, alpha rays, beta rays, X rays, and gamma rays.

Isotope: Of a collection of atoms of a given element (that is, having the same number of protons), those atoms possessing a different number of neutrons are the different isotopes of the element.

Kilohertz (kHz):   Unit of frequency.

Magnetic dipole: North and south magnetic poles, separated by a finite distance.

Magnetic field (H):   The region surrounding a magnet (or current-carrying conductor). It is endowed with certain properties; one is that a small magnet in such a region experiences a torque that tends to align it in a given direction.

Magnetic induction (B):   The net magnetic effect from an externally applied magnetic field and the resulting magnetization. Also called *magnetic flux density.*

MegaHertz (MHz):   Unit of frequency.

Neutron: A nuclear particle the size of a proton, but carrying no charge.

Nonmagnetic material: Material that cannot be magnetized.

Nuclear decay: An unstable nucleus, such as in a radioactive isotope, will attempt to reach a stable state by emitting an alpha particle or by "splitting" a proton or neutron and emitting a beta particle. In the process, its chemical identity is altered.

Nucleus: The central part of an atom containing most of the mass of the atom. It is made of protons and neutrons.

Paramagnetic material: Material that can be magnetized, but only with difficulty and only weakly.

Permeability: The ease with which a material can be magnetized or demagnetized. Substances with high permeability are easy to magnetize, and those with low permeability are hard.

Piezoelectric transducer: A device for converting electric energy into mechanical and vice versa.

Pixel: Acronym for a picture element; the smallest discrete part of a digital image display.

Positron: An unnatural particle the same size as an electron, but carrying a positive charge instead of a negative charge. This particle is manufactured in certain processes of nuclear decay and soon becomes converted to some other form of energy.

Potential difference: The energy available to move a current around an electrical circuit. It is the difference in energy between a point at a high negative potential and some other point at a low negative potential. If the two points are connected to each other, electrons will move from the high negative potential to the low; this constitutes a current flow.

Precession: Comparatively slow gyration of the axis of a spinning body so as to trace out a corner, caused by the application of a torque tending to change the direction of the rotation axis.

Proton: A nuclear particle the same size as a neutron, and carrying a positive charge. It is approximately 1,850 times larger than an electron.

Rad: A unit of radiation. The corresponding SI unit is the gray (abbreviated Gy).

Radioactive Isotope: An unstable isotope. In such an isotope, the nucleus tries to reach a stable state by the emission of a particle and, sometimes, energy.

Rem: A unit of radiation. The corresponding SI unit is the seivert (abbreviated Sv).

Roentgen: A unit of measure of an X ray; the amount of conductivity of one milliliter of atmospheric air (at saturation) at zero degrees Celsius and 760 millimeters of mercury pressure. For X rays, as used in diagnostic radiology, one roentgen equals one rad equals one rem. This relationship may not be true for other radiation sources.

SI: Abbreviation for *Système internationale d'unitès,* the system of measurements accepted by scientists worldwide. It is similar, but not identical, to the metric system.

Static discharge: When the potential difference between two electrodes separated by an insulating material becomes great enough, the surplus electrons on the negative electrode cross the gap to the positive electrode in one big burst.

Wavelength: The distance from a particular point on a wave to the same point on the next wave; for example, from the crest of one wave to the crest of the next.

X ray: A form of electromagnetic radiation.